Meditations
for
BLACK WOMEN

75 Mindful Reflections
to Help You Stay Grounded
& Find Inner Peace

Oludara Adeeyo
Bestselling Author of
Self-Care for Black Women

ADAMS MEDIA
New York   Amsterdam/Antwerp   London   Toronto   Sydney   New Delhi

Adams Media
An Imprint of Simon & Schuster, LLC
100 Technology Center Drive
Stoughton, Massachusetts 02072

First Adams Media hardcover edition
January 2025

ADAMS MEDIA and colophon are
registered trademarks of Simon &
Schuster, LLC.

For information about special discounts
for bulk purchases, please contact
Simon & Schuster Special Sales
at 1-866-506-1949 or business@
simonandschuster.com.

The Simon & Schuster Speakers Bureau
can bring authors to your live event. For
more information or to book an event,
contact the Simon & Schuster Speakers
Bureau at 1-866-248-3049 or visit our
website at www.simonspeakers.com.

Interior design by Priscilla Yuen
Illustrations by Tess Armstrong
Interior images © Simon & Schuster, LLC

Manufactured in the
United States of America

10 9 8 7 6 5 4 3 2 1

Library of Congress Cataloging-in-
Publication Data has been applied for.

ISBN 978-1-5072-2373-4
ISBN 978-1-5072-2374-1 (ebook)

*For Black women who want
to quiet their inner critic.*

Acknowledgments

Thank you to everyone who has supported my first
three books: *Self-Care for Black Women; Affirmations
for Black Women: A Journal;* and *Mind, Body, & Soul:
A Self-Care Coloring Book for Black Women.* I am
back again with another one: *Meditations for Black
Women: 75 Mindful Reflections to Help You Stay
Grounded & Find Inner Peace.* I hope you enjoy it. And
as always, thank you to everyone at Adams Media
and Simon & Schuster who worked on this project.
Your care with this subject matter is
always appreciated. Thank you.

Contents

Meditations • 17

Introduction

Meditation is a mindful exercise that encourages you to mentally slow down, release and challenge your negative thoughts, calm your inner self, and build a connection with your mind, body, and soul. If you've been feeling stressed, anxious, and disconnected from yourself, this practice can take your wellness journey to new heights! *Yes, girl.* Choosing to put yourself first by practicing mindfulness will put you on a new level of self-care. And let's be honest, you *know* you need this.

As Black women, we are often unable to quiet our inner critic; we feel forced to always work hard and have to ignore our needs to please others. Our sense of self gets lost along the way on our journey of Black womanhood. We are conditioned by the world to think that our existence is a problem, and, as a result, we think *we* are the problem. Well, no more. The road to personal healing and rejuvenation of your mind, body, and soul awaits in *Meditations for Black Women.*

Here you will learn more about the important self-care practice of self-reflection through meditation. Each of the seventy-five meditations that follows covers a subject that speaks to the experience of being a Black woman and helps you on your path to personal growth. The meditations start off with an empowering quote by a Black woman, followed by a meditation mantra, then a reflection on the subject matter, and end with a thought-provoking activity so you can integrate that meditation into your own life journey.

The meditations in this book will show you how to:

- *Break up with internalized oppression*
- *Develop your version of a balanced life*
- *Take up space*
- *Recognize your own power*
- *And more*

As you make your way through the meditations, you will be inspired to build a better relationship with yourself. After all, that is the ultimate goal of self-care.

New to meditation or still unsure of how it can help you in your personal journey? Be sure to read through the information about meditation on the next pages of this book, including its benefits and how exactly you can make it a part of your daily routine.

So get cozy, sis. A life filled with continued peace is within your reach. Let's go get it.

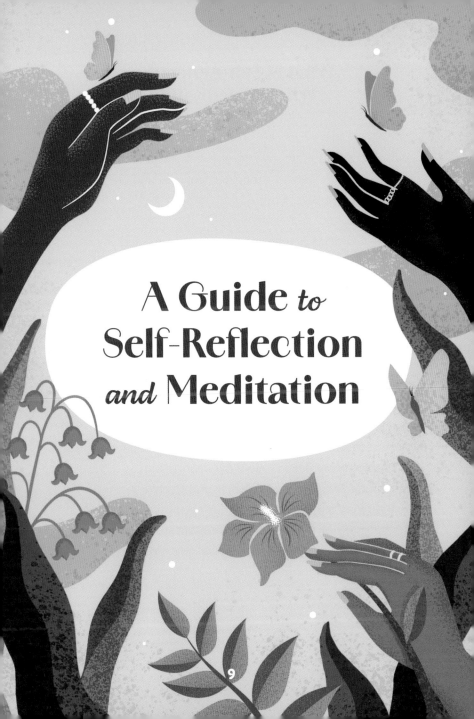

A Guide *to* Self-Reflection *and* Meditation

9

What Is Self-Reflection?
What Is Meditation?

Self-reflection is a mental exercise that includes actively look-ing inward to examine thoughts, feelings, and behaviors. Its purpose is to create a better understanding of self. Meditation itself is a form of self-reflection.

Meditation is a mental practice that is used to train the mind to focus and build awareness. Its purpose is to increase mental clarity and emotional regulation. In addition, meditation is practiced in religious and non-religious settings.

One form of meditation is mindfulness meditation. This popular meditation technique, which you will be encouraged to use as you make your way through this book, involves being present with yourself while focusing on something specific as you observe your thoughts, feelings, and other bodily sensa-tions without judgment. Mindfulness meditation creates space for you to do the work of introspection, forcing you to slow down and reconnect with your mind, body, and soul. Introspec-tion is looking within to process, heal, and grow from the effects and traumas of having to be on the receiving end of things like microaggressions and misogynoir. Misogynoir is racism and sexism that is specifically directed at Black women.

Why Is Meditation Important for Black Women?

From a young age, Black women experience discrimination that leaves a lasting impact on our self-image. Many of us weren't able to create a solid foundation for our self-esteem, because the spaces we grew up in constantly bombarded us with racist and sexist ideologies to dehumanize us. FYI: Dehumanization is at the core of a lot of the mental health issues that Black women are dealing with today. Everything about us is either questioned or criticized. Whether it be individuals, our communities, or media, we are told that everything about us goes against the ideals of society. The hair that naturally comes out of our head is unruly, the color of our skin is unappealing, the way we move through the world is disruptive, etc. And as a result, we internalize these messages and develop a poor perception of ourselves. This means that the negative beliefs you've been taking in about yourself and your community have melded to your identity. Unfortunately for us, our identity has a lot to do with how the world perceives us. Thus, you must now do the hard work of unlearning and correcting the negative thoughts you have developed about yourself, and meditation is a great place to begin this healing journey.

Additionally, research has found that meditation helps improve your mental health by improving the way you respond to psychological stress. By practicing meditation, you can better manage symptoms related to mental health disorders like anxiety and depression. There is an increase in emotional well-being and cognitive functioning, such as better self-awareness and working memory. The more you meditate, the less susceptible you are to the dangerous effects toxic stress can have on your mental and physical health. A more grounded and peaceful version of you emerges, with an improved self-image that is reflected in your thoughts, feelings, and behaviors.

Studies have also shown that forms of self-reflection like meditation can help improve cardiovascular functioning by lowering your blood pressure. This is super important as cardiovascular illnesses, like heart disease, are one of the top leading causes of death in Black women (especially in the United States). You need to be better at managing your stress levels, even if just for the sake of your physical wellness, and self-reflection can help you do that.

Before continuing, it's important to recognize that the healthcare system is not nice to Black women. Doctors constantly ignore or dismiss our medical concerns, which then usually spiral into either a wrong or late diagnosis and undertreatment or overtreatment. *Whew.* It's exhausting navigating the healthcare system as a Black woman. Sometimes, even Black doctors are not to be trusted. You may personally know that heart-wrenching disappointment of booking an appointment with a Black doctor months in advance just for them to treat you with as much disdain as a non-Black doctor. *Side eye.* The frustrating truth is that if you want to receive adequate medical care, you will have to advocate for yourself and doctor shop until you find a medical professional who will treat you like a human and listen to your health concerns. But, uh, I digress.

Ultimately, your relationship with yourself is all that matters. How you perceive yourself and how you connect with your identity has a huge impact on the connection you have with others and yourself. Choosing to practice meditation will help you repair your relationship with your mind, body, and soul. This is especially important because, as various social systems try to rattle your essence, you will need to lean more into these relationships and your capabilities of being self-assured.

How to Incorporate Moments of Meditation Into Your Life and Daily Practice

The reason you should add meditation to your everyday self-care routine is that it will encourage you to practice being present as you shift your poor self-image to a more positive one. In regard to staying present, often the cause of a lot of our anxieties and worries is that we are either pondering about the past or obsessing about the future. Choosing to include meditation in your daily wellness practice allows you to get in the habit of focusing your mind away from your stressors as you reconnect with yourself.

Here are some of the many ways that you can integrate meditation into your daily routine:

- *Use the quotes, meditation mantras, reflections, and action items in this book, and write about them in a journal. Process your thoughts around each one. Writing it down is one of the best ways to incorporate meditation into your everyday life.*

- *Choose a quote or meditation that you will focus on and think about in your quiet time. "Quiet time" here is considered five or more minutes that you devote to being still in thought and movement. As you stay focused on the quote or meditation, your body will calm your nervous system. Embrace quiet time whenever you see fit. It can be first thing in the morning, during the day, or right before bed.*

- *Select a meditation mantra that you want to focus on and say it to yourself as you exercise. Bonus points if you choose to do yoga.*

The quotes, meditation mantras, reflections, and action items that you discover in this book can be used once or as many times as you need throughout the day.

You will find that many of the meditations focus on recurring themes and offer repeated practice in these areas, such as building self-trust and seeking validation from within instead of from others. This is because sometimes we need to introduce new concepts to our minds several times so that it makes a lasting impression. These key lessons that you will learn can help you create the fulfilled, peaceful, and joyous life you deserve.

How to Find Inspiration and Power from Other Black Women

Each meditation page in this book is led by a quote from an empowering Black woman public figure. From authors to politicians, to activists to artists and scientists, you will find a quote from a Black woman that will hopefully have you feeling inspired and empowered.

To find inspiration from these quotes, think about who these women are and all the obstacles they had to endure to get to the position they now hold or once held. The road to success for a Black woman is filled with a lot of speed bumps, potholes, and broken bridges. But what a lot of the women whose quotes you will embrace have in common is their resilience. *I know, I know. We're not fans of that word in our community.* We've dropped the "strong Black woman" trope. We're all in our soft era. However, the truth is that a lot of the Black women we admire, dead or alive, had to go through some *reaaal stuff* to get to their level of success and wisdom.

So, we honor their lives, legacies, and bravery for paving the way for future generations of Black women. Let us follow in their footsteps and enjoy the words of wisdom that they have to share with the masses. Let their words empower you as you practice the meditations in this book and through every step of your journey to your happiest, healthiest life.

Meditations

Focus On Yourself

> **It's important, therefore, to know who the real enemy is, and to know the function, the very serious function of racism, which is distraction. It keeps you from doing your work. It keeps you explaining over and over again, your reason for being.**

TONI MORRISON, author, "A Humanistic View" speech
at Portland State University in 1975

MEDITATION

I will not allow racism to distract
me from pursuing my dreams.

REFLECTION

It's true. Racism (and sexism; *hello*, misogynoir) exists to distract you from what's really important: becoming the best version of yourself in this lifetime. And the best way to get there is by living life with less stress and more rest. Experiencing things like discrimination and prejudice because of your racial and gender identity creates emotional distress that can be detrimental to the mind, body, and soul.

For example, you may find yourself caught up in trying to make sense of microaggressive stings in the workplace, such as questioning your self-worth because you're being paid less than your non-Black colleagues, becoming physically ill from stress because you're being held back from or overlooked for yet another promotion, or finding yourself frustrated because your coworkers are committed to misunderstanding you. And while it is certainly tempting to try to understand why you're facing mistreatment at work, it is not your job to figure out why others do you wrong all because you are a Black woman.

You see, when you are constantly dealing with the wounds of racism-related stress, you will not have enough time to pursue your dreams or manifest a life that you feel aligns with who you are as a person. This is exactly how oppressive systems operate. They steal from our cultures and ask us, Black women, to overextend ourselves and prove to people who enjoy upholding these demeaning societal structures why we are worthy of being seen as human and deserving of a place in this world.

So, sis, do not allow the systems of oppression to get in the way of your destiny.

Take Action

Reflect on ways you can soothe yourself emotionally when dealing with microaggressions.

Add Rest to Your Activism

❝ Anyone who's interested in making change in the world also has to learn how to take care of herself, himself, theirselves. ❞

ANGELA DAVIS, political activist, in a 2018 interview with *AFROPUNK*

MEDITATION

The best way I can help change the world is by taking care of myself.

REFLECTION

Black women seem to always be at the forefront of helping to enact change in and outside of our communities across the globe. We help start movements, we encourage systematic shifts, and we advocate for justice. If this describes who you are, then you need to make sure that self-care is part of your activism. After all, rest is a form of resistance (shout-out to Tricia Hersey).

You see, it may feel like in order to witness the change you want to see in the world, you need to keep grinding and ignoring your needs. However, you cannot pour strength and hope into others if your wellness cup is empty. Your mental, physical, and spiritual well-being is an important element in fighting for the social causes that you care about. A pushback against society's desire for you to sacrifice yourself for the greater good is necessary. The work you do for your communities should come from a place of rest.

Not sure how you can do that? Don't worry. It takes practice to make sure your activism includes rest. Start by creating boundaries around what you care about. For example: Limit how much daily information you consume on the social issues close to your heart. This can look like not getting on social media first thing in the morning (or right before bed) to see the struggles and tragedies others are going through. Starting your day off (or ending your day) with a bit of trauma is not good for your nervous system. It can keep you hypervigilant and exacerbate any underlying mental health problems.

Take Action
Think about how you can include rest and other self-care practices in your daily routine while also participating in social causes you care about.

Don't Be Discouraged by Life's Setbacks

> ❝ *We may encounter many defeats,*
> *but we must not be defeated.* ❞

MAYA ANGELOU, author, to *The Paris Review* in 1990

MEDITATION

Sometimes life's disappointments will knock me out, but I must get up and keep going.

REFLECTION

Fact: Life is hard. You will go through trials and tribulations, but you must not let these disappointments and failures define who you are or your future. *I know, easier said than done*, especially when there are various disparities in this world that impact Black women at a higher rate (e.g., the wage pay gap and health inequities).

Let's be real. Moving through this world on a regular basis with its normal stressors, while having to deal with things like microaggressions and other effects of systemic oppression, is exhausting. So when something like losing a job, ending a relationship, or burying a loved one unexpectedly happens, it feels like a punch to the gut. It can rightfully leave you feeling hopeless, anxious, and uncertain about your future endeavors. You might even find it hard to make your next life decisions, paralyzed by feelings like fear and anger.

However, pushing past these emotions is something you absolutely can and must do. You don't have to let being systematically denied access to things like higher wages, equitable healthcare, and better education stop you from pursuing the aforementioned. Find the right support, such as a trusted friend, family member, or mental health professional. You will need safe spaces and people to help you feel encouraged to move forward after facing devastating setbacks. This will prevent you from internalizing whatever negative narrative you may be telling yourself about your recent disappointment. You are not what has happened to you. Your defeats do not define you; you define you.

Take Action

Who in your life can help you through life's setbacks?
Reach out and thank them for their support.
And if you can't think of anybody, begin
brainstorming who that could be.

Make Your Own Life Decisions

> **❝** *I will not have my life narrowed down.*
> *I will not bow down to somebody else's whim*
> *or to someone else's ignorance.* **❞**

bell hooks, author, *Ain't I a Woman: Black Women and Feminism*

MEDITATION

What other people think about my life decisions is none of my business.

REFLECTION

People will always have their own beliefs about how you should be living your life. From family members to friends to coworkers, somebody will always have their own opinion on what they think is best for you, especially if you are a Black woman. It's like everybody always wants to be in our business. You'll have to learn to shake that off and make decisions that feel true to you.

You see, many of us come from families where the previous generations had to deal with actual laws and limitations (e.g., Jim Crow laws and redlining in the United States). Having to make life decisions based on where you were "allowed" to go as a Black person will, in fact, alter your psyche and the way you see yourself and your future capabilities. This creates a scarcity mindset—the belief that you will always have limited resources. As a result, this thinking is sometimes passed down to the next generation through judgment and critique of life decisions.

But it is a new era. We are in a time period where you are capable of living the life of your wildest dreams. You just have to believe that you can and start working toward it by making life decisions that feel aligned with your spirit. Here are some ways you can do this:

- *Learn to ignore opinions from others that fill you with self-doubt.*
- *Limit sharing plans with those whose opinions fill you with self-doubt.*
- *Find people who encourage you to think big or differently.*
- *Stop comparing your life's journey to your peers.*

Take Action

Explore with yourself if there are any big or small life decisions you've been holding off on completing because of other people's opinions.

Learn to Trust Yourself

" *You can't be hesitant about who you are.* "

VIOLA DAVIS, actor, producer, to *Playbill* in 2004

MEDITATION

I trust that I can handle anything
that comes my way.

REFLECTION

Hard truth: Lacking self-trust usually means you have a poor
self-image. Let's talk about it.

First off, your self-image is how you see, think, and feel
about yourself. There's no doubt that learning to trust yourself
is a hard journey to navigate. However, as a Black woman, it is
something you absolutely have to practice. Having self-trust will
help you through the hardest moments in your life, especially
as the surrounding society tries to dehumanize you by pushing
negative stereotypes and limited beliefs on to you, asking you
to abandon your true self and relinquish your self-agency.

For example, perhaps you have been or currently are in
relationships (romantic, platonic, work, etc.) where the other individuals do not make you feel safe to fully show up as yourself.
(Let's be real. The world doesn't really make folks with melanin

feel safe anywhere. But, I digress.) Hiding parts of who you are or conceding to the emotional or physical needs of others— ahem, people pleasing—is not good for your well-being. You develop the habit of ignoring your needs and wants to the point of emotional numbness and loss of self-understanding. Knowing who you are is your greatest power, and that intimidates people who want you to think less of yourself.

To get better at trusting yourself, you must first have self-compassion because this is learned thinking and behavior that will not change overnight. Next, get to know yourself by honoring your intuition and voice. (Check out the Trust Your Intuition meditation for guidance in honoring your intuition and voice.) Let these be the guiding light in your decision-making. When you stand tall in your convictions, you increase your self-confidence. Lastly, give yourself permission to believe that you can handle any tough emotion or situation that comes your way in the future.

Take Action
Brainstorm some ways that you can show yourself compassion as you work on trusting yourself more.

Prioritize Your Self-Care

*" Caring for myself is not self-indulgence,
it is self-preservation, and that is an
act of political warfare. "*

AUDRE LORDE, author, *A Burst of Light and Other Essays*

MEDITATION

I understand that practicing self-care is an
important part of my wellness journey.

REFLECTION

Now more than ever, it is imperative that you recognize stress has a significant impact on your overall well-being. To combat the toxicity of stress, you must be proactive in your own self-preservation, your own self-care.

Don't know where to start? I gotchu. Ya girl who wrote this book that you're currently reading is a self-care aficionado. Self-care is not just about manicures and massages; it's about doing the internal work that will help you align your life with your true self. The better you take care of yourself, the better you will feel about yourself, and it will reflect in your external life. In this guide, you will find practical ways to start including self-care in your everyday life, because what starts practical will become instinctual. *Mwah.*

Let us digress. As a Black woman, choosing to put yourself first will be seen as a betrayal by others in and around your life. The world calls for Black women to be martyrs for the well-being of society, historically and currently. However, you do not need to do all that. It is not your job to save everybody but yourself. You must first take care of yourself so you can take care of others. And if you don't want to take care of anyone else, that's cool too.

All in all, prioritizing your needs is in fact an act of political warfare. It disrupts the way the world wants you to live and shifts you into a space of true peace. No longer will you care about the expectations of others when it comes to your existence as a Black woman. Through your wellness journey, you will gain a deeper understanding of yourself. You will enjoy simply being you.

Take Action

What is one activity you can do today that will help you prioritize your self-care and better manage your stress? Go do it.

"Caring for myself is not self-indulgence, it is *self-preservation*, and that is an act of *political warfare.*"

AUDRE LORDE,
author, *A Burst of Light and Other Essays*

Break Up with
Internalized Oppression

**❝ *We must cease being participants
in our own oppression.* ❞**

STACEY ABRAMS, politician, lawyer, voting rights activist, author

MEDITATION

How the world perceives me does not
have to align with how I see me.

REFLECTION

Internalized oppression is when you attach your self-image to
the negative stereotypes perpetuated in society about your
marginalized community. This can look like believing you are
not worthy of experiencing upward mobility in life because, historically, your people have been dehumanized, othered, and
ostracized. As a result, your feelings and behaviors mimic this
belief. You might find yourself having low self-esteem and thinking that you deserve less than others.

Here's another example: Statistically, Black women are less
likely to be married, and the media does not let us forget it. *My
gawd.* There are articles, podcasts, TV shows, etc., about how

we are more single than ever, and it's allegedly because we are less desirable. *Lies.* So, if you are constantly consuming these messages, you will begin to believe they are true. Combined with the push of Eurocentric beauty standards, you will think that you are the problem and create a poor relationship with yourself. You are not the problem. Misogynoir is the problem.

Breaking up with internalized oppression will require intention and self-compassion. You've been brainwashed and will have to actively let go of any thoughts tied to white supremacy. This includes no longer holding yourself or your community to a degrading standard that was created by them white folks. *Ta ta, respectability politics.*

The journey of releasing your self-oppressive beliefs will help you call back your power and increase your self-confidence. So, get started. First, examine any thoughts you have that feel negative about your intersecting identities. Ask yourself why you think this, and then challenge these thoughts with positive reframes or positive affirmations.

Take Action

Be honest with yourself. Explore and challenge any internalized oppressive beliefs you have about yourself as a Black woman.

Embrace Life's Imperfections

> *I realized that I don't have to be perfect. All I have to do is show up and enjoy the messy, imperfect, and beautiful journey of my life.*

KERRY WASHINGTON, actor, producer, director

My life does not require me to be perfect for it to be enjoyable.

Embracing life's imperfections can be hard, but it's how you can live a beautiful life. You are more than likely a high achiever, accomplishing great things and asking for greatness in all areas of your life in the name of Black excellence. But, girl. At what cost? Let's talk about it. The truth is, the world makes you feel like if you want to be treated right, you must be the perfect Black woman. Follow all the rules, achieve all the goals, get all the degrees, make all the money, wear all the right clothes, etc. But, in a world that does not value melanated bodies, you can be perfect on paper and still receive disrespect and discrimination.

That's why it is time to release the pressure of perfectionism from your life. It is no longer serving you. Matter of fact, it is probably one of the reasons you may be having trouble managing your stress. The root of perfectionism is anxiety and a lack of self-trust. You have likely convinced yourself that, in order for your life to be enjoyable, everything must go according to your perfect plan. And if we're being real, life is gonna life and do what it wants despite your preparation.

To cut ties with the idea that you must be perfect to obtain good things, you will have to shift your mindset about yourself and embrace life's imperfections. This means trying new things and failing, sitting in the uncomfortable feelings of uncertainty, and practicing letting go of needing to control every aspect of your life.

Take Action

Envision what embracing the imperfect parts of your life would look like to you.

Recognize Your Own Power

> ❝ *The most common way people give up their power is by thinking they don't have any.* ❞
>
> ALICE WALKER, author, activist

MEDITATION

No one can take my power away from me without my permission.

REFLECTION

Recognizing your own power is an exercise in speaking your truth and having the courage to face adversity head-on. This is a radical act, because you are in a world where Black women are silenced, ignored, and forced to dim their light so it doesn't shine too bright in other people's eyes. *Well, it is your time to shine!*

Conditioned into thinking that you do not have any power, you must now recognize that it is the exact opposite. Society has lied to you. Having power is understanding that you always have a choice in this life. That means the strength to navigate the complexities of your life have always lived within you. They just needed to be awakened. Quite frankly, your ability to be powerful is ancestral. You come from a long line of

Black women and men who had to endure societal hardships and managed to be resourceful despite inadequate resources, but still created a life for themselves. No matter where your Black ancestry originates from (in or outside the United States), your ancestors lived through the effects of colonization. Being able to overcome things like enslavement and genocide to experience civil rights creates a bloodline filled with strong and resourceful individuals.

To start embracing that you are a powerful person, you must first acknowledge your uniqueness. It is vital that you realize only you can be emboldened to use your prowess however you want for your benefit. You can start small by creating boundaries and telling the people who love you "no" when you don't feel like doing something.

Ultimately, using your voice and speaking your truth is how you reclaim your power. An exercise like this will call for you to change the way you think about yourself by challenging negative thoughts that make you feel helpless. Release the anxiety. Yes, it is scary to use your power to speak up for yourself (and others), but you gotta do it. It is a pivotal part of your self-care journey.

Take Action

Think about how you can step further into your power in both a small and big way. What would that look like for you?

Connect with Your Softness

❝ I have chosen to no longer be apologetic for my femaleness and my femininity. And I want to be respected in all of my femaleness because I deserve to be. ❞

CHIMAMANDA NGOZI ADICHIE, Nigerian author, in her 2013 TEDx Talk, "We Should All Be Feminists"

MEDITATION

However I choose to express my femininity is valid.

REFLECTION

Connecting with your softness and femininity is a revolutionary act, especially in a world that expects Black women to remain strong and resilient at all times. Let's not forget that if a woman has dark brown skin, wide hips, and some *Jackson 5 nostrils*, people will call her masculine because she does not fit into the Eurocentric beauty standard of being thin and lighter-skinned, with petite facial features. *Booo!*

To be feminine is to be you. If you identify as a woman, you are automatically feminine and have a right to claim the softness of your womanhood. Traditional femininity is associated with socially constructed female traits, such as nurturing, gentleness, and grace. And by embracing your femaleness, you are rejecting the idea that your self-worth is tied to your ability to remain tough and steadfast in the midst of hardships.

Your ability to engage with your softness is your strength because you are defining femininity for yourself. It takes courage to lean into the gentle side of yourself, despite dealing with things like racism and sexism that aim to break you down and make you build up a tough emotional wall. Softness is your feminine right. Allow yourself to exist in this tender space by practicing self-compassion and self-acceptance. Determine what being soft looks like to you by spending time with yourself, doing activities that bring out your sweet side and make you feel joyful and free.

When Tupac Shakur said, "the blacker the berry, the sweeter the juice," he was most definitely talking about us, sisters.

Take Action

How can you connect with your softer side? Go do that.

Leave Your Comfort Zone

❝ There will be people who say to you, 'You are out of your lane.' They are burdened by only having the capacity to see what has always been instead of what can be. But don't you let that burden you. ❞

KAMALA HARRIS, first Black Vice President of the United States, at the 2020 Black Girls Lead conference

MEDITATION

Outside of my comfort zone are endless opportunities.

REFLECTION

Leaving your comfort zone allows you to open the door to endless opportunities. A comfort zone is a state in which your thoughts and behaviors consistently operate at the same level. This is because the environment you are in is low-risk. When you are in this mental or physical space, there is no motivation to try new things. While comfort zones provide you with a safe place to self-regulate and establish routine, learning to step outside of that low-risk territory is beneficial to your self-care journey.

Escaping your comfort zone is absolutely scary if you don't do it often. However, it will ignite your journey of self-discovery and personal growth. You will learn to embrace your authentic self, redefine your capabilities, and broaden your self-perspective. Additionally, you will develop the ability to thrive in unfamiliar environments without excessive fear or anxiety. Often, we are afraid of leaving our comfort zone because we are influenced by others and their own anxieties and fears. It's time to silence the nay-sayers and stay focused on your new path.

To begin the process of leaving the confines of your comfort zone, you will have to first examine areas in your life where you crave growth. Determine if you are operating in or outside of your comfort zone in these areas. Then, explore the why and how you can shift the way you move in these particular areas. Remember, going outside of your comfort zone doesn't always have to be some grand gesture. It can be tiny steps you make toward what you want to change. In addition, you will also have to practice positive self-talk to counteract any opposing opinions that have influenced your thoughts on your capabilities to step into unknown territory in your life.

You deserve better, always. And once you realize countless chances for success are outside of your comfort zone, you will be unstoppable.

Take Action
What is one way you can live life outside your comfort zone this week? Try it.

Find Your Joy

❝ You have to find what sparks a light in you so that you in your own way can illuminate the world. ❞

OPRAH WINFREY, media mogul, talk show host,
actor, producer, philanthropist

MEDITATION

Choosing to chase my joy will lead me to a fulfilled life.

REFLECTION

Finding your joy in a world that often overlooks Black women is a revolutionary act of self-love and self-preservation. Cultivating happiness is what helps you unearth your life's purpose, reclaim your personal narrative, and build self-confidence that illuminates the world.

To find what brings you joy, you will have to go on a journey of self-discovery. To maintain your joy, you will have to be intentional about engaging with the things that make your soul smile. Knowing what joy looks like to you is important because what brings everyone joy is unique to their liking.

Joy can be found in different ways. It can be found in simple pleasures like long walks and listening to your favorite song on repeat, or through shared experiences like finding a community and sisterhood of friends who share your interests and empower each other. In a society that wants to see you suffer, your joy is a declaration that your existence is not defined by your struggles, but by the bright light that lives within you. The path to true joy starts with prioritizing your self-care and mental health. You will need to set boundaries with the people in your life and seek additional support when you need it. Creating joy in your life also begins with speaking positively to yourself and challenging any negative thoughts that seek to ruin your happiness.

Take Action

Take a moment to think about what brings you joy. Then plan how you can make more time for these things.

Develop Unshakable Self-Confidence

> *Sometimes, I feel discriminated against, but it does not make me angry. It merely astonishes me. How can any deny themselves the pleasure of my company? It's beyond me.*

ZORA NEALE HURSTON, author, in "How It Feels to Be Colored Me"

MEDITATION

The pain and confusion from the discrimination I feel does not overpower my self-confidence.

REFLECTION

Truth be told, it hurts to be on the receiving end of misogynoir. Because of someone else's internal biases, they can decide that you, being a Black woman, calls for you to receive malicious treatment. As a result, you experience discrimination that can create tangible and intangible barriers to success. It's actually pretty astonishing, just like Zora Neale Hurston said, and if you really think about it...it makes no sense.

That's because you are more than your physical identities. Your personality and other characteristics matter the most. Are you kind, trustworthy, and honest in relationships with others? Do people find you pleasant to be around? *This* is what others should care about, not the color of your skin or your gender.

And while experiencing prejudices, like being told you can't wear your hair naturally at work or school, causes you pain and confusion, you must develop unshakable self-confidence. This will ensure that you are not rattled by the negative things people say or assume about you. Let them sit in their funky thoughts. Having immovable assurance about who you are as a person is what will help you progress further in this world. You will become unstoppable as you blossom into who you are because self-confidence breeds alignment with yourself and the world around you.

To develop steadfast confidence, you must get to know yourself. This can look like completing activities alone, creating deeper relationships with people you trust, making decisions without anyone's input, and accomplishing small goals, like tidying up your living space. Need help with developing skills that will help you have confidence? Check out the Reclaim Control of Your Life, Understand Your Self-Worth, and Follow Your Conscience meditations in this book.

Take Action

If your self-esteem is low, think of a small goal that you know you can achieve and go do it. You'll feel better about yourself.

"Sometimes, I feel discriminated against, but it does not make me angry. It merely astonishes me. It merely astonishes me. How can any deny themselves the *pleasure* of my *company?* It's beyond me."

ZORA NEALE HURSTON, author, in "How It Feels to Be Colored Me"

Overcome Self-Doubt

" Don't underestimate yourself. You are more capable than you think. "

MISTY COPELAND, American ballet dancer

MEDITATION

Instead of doubting myself, I choose to think that I am capable of doing anything.

REFLECTION

Being able to overcome self-doubt is a big deal. It is essential to your personal growth journey because of the unique challenges you face in your everyday life: the microaggressions, the hypervisibility from possibly being the only Black woman in different settings, and the sadness and loneliness that comes with being othered. As the world frequently undermines your painful lived experiences, you have to deal with systemic and individual obstacles created by racist and sexist ideologies. Additionally, stereotypes about your intersecting identities are often ingrained in you through false and biased representations.

To conquer self-doubt, you must work on the internal narrative you have about yourself by building up your self-confidence. Learning to trust your voice, instincts, and choices will be a key part of this journey. You can do this by first embracing your identity and acknowledging your strengths. (Read or revisit the Recognize Your Inner Magic and Find Your Voice meditations for more guidance.) It's okay to take a second or two to evaluate your dynamic characteristics. You are *that girl*.

Next, find like-minded individuals who are going to empower you and be a supportive community around you. Sharing life experiences and learning from other people's journeys will help you create a sense of belonging. You will receive the exact kind of validation you need to peel back the layers of self-doubt that are holding you back. Need help figuring out how to tap into your community for healing? Check out the Ask for Help and Use Your Support Systems meditations for more guidance.

Most importantly, you will need to set tiny, attainable goals that will help you build momentum as you prove your capabilities to yourself. Throughout this process, you must be staying present with yourself and actively challenging your negative thoughts with positive reframes or affirmations. Get some encouragement to release negative thoughts by visiting the Let Your Light Shine meditation. Overcoming self-doubt is a continuous journey that requires patience and self-compassion, but you can rise above it and thrive.

Take Action

What's one attainable goal can you set that will help you get the ball rolling on releasing self-doubt?

Stay Motivated to Reach Your Goals

" I don't focus on what I'm up against. I focus on my goals, and I try to ignore the rest. "

VENUS WILLIAMS, American professional tennis player, in a 2008 CNN interview

My goals are within my reach and I will not be intimidated by the journey.

Finding motivation in the face of systemic inequalities and societal pressures requires courage and a strong sense of self-assuredness. Many things can easily discourage your desire to stay the path toward your goals. It could be behavioral (lack of planning or motivation) or it could be biological (a mental or physical illness). Pro tip: If you suspect your inability to stay motivated might be due to psychiatric reasons, such as a mental illness or an executive function disorder, please see a healthcare professional, like a primary care doctor or a mental health therapist, for further assessment and to receive the extra support you may need. Knowing what's going on inside your mind and body is just as important as making self-guided behavioral modifications that will improve your ability to stay motivated. Nevertheless, it is important to remember that your journey to success ultimately relies on you.

To maintain the momentum of motivation, you have to decide what success looks like to you. Comparison is the thief of joy, so the way you choose to measure your accomplishments must be distinct to you—not what you may be witnessing in other people's lives close to you or on social media. (Also, a social media break wouldn't hurt during this time period.) Use the Define Success for Yourself meditation later in this book to dig deeper into what success looks like and means to you.

Additionally, the following will also help you stay motivated: a community that supports you, a self-care routine that prioritizes your needs, and an intentional meditative practice of challenging your negative thoughts. All in all, it's about focusing less on the barriers and distractions to your goals and more on how you can reach them.

Take Action

Reflect on ways you can remove the things that distract you from reaching your goals.

Create Opportunities for Yourself

« Don't sit down and wait for the opportunities to come. Get up and make them. »

MADAM C.J. WALKER, American entrepreneur, philanthropist, activist

MEDITATION

I create opportunities for myself;
I don't wait for them.

REFLECTION

Creating opportunities for yourself as a Black woman is how you push back against a society that desires to dictate your progress and refuse you access to other avenues for growth and success. If someone is going to place a barrier between you and your goals, then it is your right to walk, run, or jump around that obstacle and find a different path to your desired end result.

Being able to create opportunities for yourself is an ancestral right. You descend from individuals who had to be inventive with how they lived their lives. Whether they were enslaved or lacked adequate resources, our ancestors were ingenious enough to overcome their limited means to do things like provide for their families or simply eat (look it up: origins of chitterlings, a.k.a. chitlins).

Nevertheless, we are now in the twenty-first century, where finding opportunities is a bit more accessible but still not that easy to do. Finding new paths to success requires a combination of self-determination, strategic thinking, risk-taking, and social support. You will have to invest in your education and skill development, which can look like getting another degree or learning something in a more cost-effective manner like reading a book or taking an online course. The point is, refining your craft will help open doors to new opportunities. Advocating for yourself will be a crucial part of your strategy. This can be through networking with others or promoting yourself in spaces like the Internet.

Ultimately, embracing going outside your comfort zone (see the Leave Your Comfort Zone meditation earlier in this book) will help you navigate the challenges of carving out paths to success in your chosen endeavors.

Take Action

Brainstorm ways you can create new opportunities for yourself to reach your goals.

Start Over after You've Failed

I really think a champion is defined not by their wins but by how they can recover when they fall.

SERENA WILLIAMS, American former professional tennis player

MEDITATION

My failures do not define me for I will always try again.

REFLECTION

Starting over after you've failed is a disheartening yet empowering journey, especially as a Black woman, because we live in a world that does not allow us to fail, nor does it grant us the opportunity to gracefully bounce back from our mistakes. Black women are always held to a different standard. Society would rather have us suffer forever from our missteps than see us win, but that does not have to be your story.

You are allowed to have a fresh start after a setback. While expectations from loved ones or society may try to bind you to your past disappointments, it is imperative that you learn to break free from these restrictions. Embrace your failures as a stepping stone toward growth. This is a normal and character-defining part of your life's story.

But, uh, where do you even begin when you want to start over? Well, first, you will have to acknowledge your emotions and give yourself the time and space to heal. Seek out support from people you trust or a mental health professional to change the negative self-image you may have developed because of this failure. Then, when you're ready, reflect on the lessons that you learned from it. Use what you've learned as the foundation to your renewed journey to success.

Starting over after you've failed is about defining success on your own terms, not what your mama or daddy says—heck, not even what you may have been taught in restrictive spaces like school or church. You have to channel your disappointment into rebuilding a future that aligns with your ambitions. Being able to do this will help increase your self-confidence because you will see how much power you have in rewriting your own story. Go hit that refresh button on your life, sis.

Take Action

If you are in a space where you need to start over, what is stopping you from doing so? Reflect on this.

Speak Up for Yourself

" _When I liberate myself, I liberate others. If you don't speak out, ain't nobody going to speak out for you._ "

FANNIE LOU HAMER, American civil rights activist

MEDITATION

Choosing to speak up for myself gives others permission to do the same.

REFLECTION

Learning to speak up for yourself is crucial for your well-being as a Black woman. This is because history shows that when Black women start talking, people listen then mobilize, and systems of oppression begin to unravel. And the powers that be (racist white folks) would prefer if we just—_shhh_—be quiet. Not. Going. To. Happen.

Speaking up forces you to practice being assertive. It's empowering to use your voice to inspire people and bring positive change to your community. Your voice holds the power to disrupt the systems that exist and create a path for future generations to do the same. If it weren't for previous voices like Fannie Lou Hamer, there wouldn't have been political advancement in the civil rights movement for Black people living in

Mississippi. She used her voice to make changes, and you can too. Ms. Hamer was also right: If you don't speak up for yourself and your community, who will?

There's no doubt that speaking up for yourself and others can be challenging and scary. Black people have also been punished for using their voices. However, it is through practicing speaking up that you will increase your self-confidence and reclaim your power. To start speaking up for yourself, you can assert your voice with people you trust. The more you do it, the more comfortable you will get with speaking up about anything. Your voice matters, and it's time to use it.

Take Action

Do you struggle with speaking up for yourself? If so, explore why you find it hard to assert yourself.

Live for Yourself

" If you don't live your life, then who will? "

RIHANNA, singer, actor, businesswoman

MEDITATION

I must learn to live my life for
me and nobody else.

REFLECTION

Living for yourself and nobody else is an act of self-liberation. Really think about the quote provided in this meditation, and ask yourself, *Who am I living for? Me or somebody else?* Sometimes we don't even know that we are living for other people. That somebody else in question could be your family, societal standards, or followers on social media. If you feel like this might be you, then it is time for you to start prioritizing your desires or dreams.

Choosing to live for yourself is a form of resistance in a world that is constantly trying to force Black women to live according to some cockamamie societal standards—standards that don't serve a purpose other than to make individuals who don't live up to them feel bad about the pace of their lives. The truth is your life's timeline is perfect how it is. However slow or fast you move into different stages of life (e.g., career, marriage, parenthood, etc.) is nobody else's business. You are the one who gets to decide what you want to do with your life, and no one should make you doubt or second-guess the essence of your life.

To embark on this empowering journey of self-discovery to living for yourself, it is essential that you learn the importance of validating yourself. Yes, it is okay to get forms of external validation through people and things, but you must be able to affirm yourself. You can do this by actively challenging any thoughts of self-doubt or low self-worth. (Read the Understand Your Self-Worth meditation for further guidance.) All in all, when you start prioritizing your needs, you honor your authentic self and your wellness journey.

Take Action

Do you think you are living for yourself or somebody else? Reflect on this and think about ways you can either begin to or continue to live for yourself.

Seek Out Sacred Spaces

*" You deserve safety. You deserve protection.
You deserve love. You deserve peace. "*

TARANA BURKE, founder of the #MeToo Movement,
in *You Are Your Best Thing: Vulnerability, Shame
Resilience, and the Black Experience*

MEDITATION

The only spaces I should be in are
those that are filled with peace.

REFLECTION

It is okay to seek out places that feel safe for you to completely be yourself as a Black woman. These are called sacred spaces, which can be the comfort of your own bedroom or home, in a community environment, or with a loved one. Safety isn't just about being protected physically; it's also about guarding your mental health from unnecessary stressors. That's what racism and sexism are: unneeded stressors. As you navigate this world, you know that you will encounter emotionally stressful environments. However, you have the choice to not share space with people who do things that invalidate your existence.

You deserve to be in community with people who validate the good and bad that come with your lived experience.

Furthermore, sacred spaces are important for Black women because these gatherings are where you will find support from kinfolk, foster a sense of belonging, and not have to deal with things like microaggressions or misogynoir. You will improve your mental well-being and maintain your inner peace. Spaces where you feel safe, heard, and loved can be with your closest circle of friends, an in-person or virtual support group, or other culture-related gatherings. Sometimes, it can even be just one person that you consider your sacred space.

However, it can be hard to find this type of solace for yourself. Perhaps you live in an area with few Black people or you have a busy schedule that doesn't allow frequent social events. Sacred spaces are not limited to just kinfolk. You can also find peace with individuals who are not Black. These are people who are willing to see you as a human being and not just as your intersecting identities. Either way, knowing how to seek out sacred spaces is essential to your wellness journey.

Take Action

Do you have a sacred space? Who, what, or where is it? If you don't have a sacred space, think about how you can find or create one for yourself.

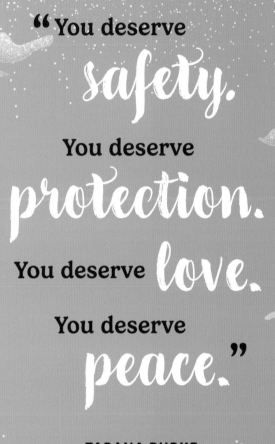

"You deserve *safety.*

You deserve *protection.*

You deserve *love.*

You deserve *peace.*"

TARANA BURKE,
founder of the #MeToo Movement,
in *You Are Your Best Thing: Vulnerability,
Shame Resilience, and the Black Experience*

Believe in Your Dreams

> **No matter where you are from,
> your dreams are valid.**

LUPITA NYONG'O, actor, in her 2014 Oscar acceptance speech

MEDITATION

I must continue to believe in my dreams
even if they seem unbelievable.

REFLECTION

When it comes to having big dreams, Black women are the queens of this. Not only are we high achievers, we are dream crushers. As the world overlooks our aspirations, we do not. We remain steadfast and push forward toward the goalpost. There is not a goal that we usually do not meet, especially when it comes to education and career. We*clap*make*clap*moves.

But the truth is, believing in yourself and your goals is easier said than done. The structure of the world conditions you to think that what you want is not within your reach. There is a lack of representation for Black women in many industries. Often, Black women have to be the one to pave the way for the next sista. *The first.* And sometimes, we're bystanders to others having lived experiences that we could only imagine—like getting a job with no related experience. However, the reason to continue believing in your dreams is that it helps you foster a better relationship with your inner being.

You see, when you have something to be hopeful for, you act differently, like creating tiny goals to get you closer to your wildest dreams. You become more motivated in the process, relinquishing any self-doubt about your skills and capability. Self-determination becomes your first name. But sometimes, as you're pursuing your dreams, it can feel like you are going nowhere. Don't be discouraged. It is always better to be prepared for when your dreams finally come into fruition. You won't mess up your blessing. You'll be successful.

Take Action

What is your wildest dream and what are you doing to work toward it? Think of something small that you can do this week to get closer to that dream.

Plan for Your Dreams

Dreams become reality when we put our minds to it.

QUEEN LATIFAH, rapper, actor, singer

MEDITATION

Preparation is an important part of seeing my dreams come to fruition.

REFLECTION

Planning for your goals is the key to achieving success. When the time comes for you to fulfill your dreams, you want to be prepared. Being prepared plus having an opportunity will equal success!

Preparation for your goals also lets the universe or your god know that you are serious about your dreams. In return, your higher power usually answers with an opportunity. So, if an opportunity dropped in your lap to fulfill your wildest dreams today, would you be prepared to jump on it and complete the goals you want in this life? If not, now is when you need to start planning.

To prepare for achieving your dreams, you've got to come up with a plan. First, let go of any thoughts that may be blocking you from believing you can reach your goals. Then write down what your goals are. Next, come up with a strategy or plan that will put you closer to fulfilling your desired accomplishments. Finally, take tiny, actionable steps toward that goal.

For example, let's say your dream is to move to a different state or country. You wouldn't just decide to one day pack up your stuff and leave to a new place without any preparation. Your prep would include research, exploration, and proper planning to ensure a smooth move. It's the same with any goals you have. You have to put your mind to it and prepare.

Take Action

Do you think you are well-prepared to work toward your goals? If not, what can you do to get closer to being ready?

Work with What's in Front of You

ZENDAYA, actor, singer

MEDITATION

Focusing on my strengths will
help me reach my goals.

REFLECTION

When it comes to reaching your goals, it is best to be resourceful and work with your strengths—working with what you've got right in front of you. This means that the best way to start working toward the things you want to accomplish is to start with what you have access to right now. This practice requires you to become present rather than be solely future thinking.

Working with what you got (like your current skills) can be a stepping stone that helps you get closer to your goals. Improvising and doing what you can with what you got is what we and our people have been doing for centuries. For Black women, this is definitely our strength.

Additionally, when it comes to working with what you got, baby girl, remember that you are Black and that means you already understand there may be barriers to success that are beyond your control and have nothing to do with your concerted efforts.

Now, to get good and be present and understand your strengths and weaknesses when it comes to reaching your goals, you have got to spend quiet time with yourself. Quiet time can be five or more minutes that you devote to being still with your thoughts and emotions. Really assess all of your current capabilities and go from there.

Take Action

Explore your goals and think about the first step you can take toward achieving them while working with what you've got. What strengths can you use to start moving toward your goals?

Find Fulfilling Work

KATHERINE JOHNSON, NASA mathematician

MEDITATION

I am allowed to enjoy the work
that I do for a living.

REFLECTION

Pursuing a career that brings you joy and fulfillment can have a significant impact on your overall well-being. The workplace is one of the main spaces that we as Black women spend most of our days. It's where you may experience things like microaggressions, discrimination, bullying, and other things that jab at your existence. So, if you have to put up with the mess that is your day job, you're better off actually liking what you do for a living, especially if you don't like the people you work with. *Ha.*

So, one of the hardest things about living in a capitalist society is that often, many people don't have a choice to do work that they like. Everybody is just trying to survive—and let's be real, there's nothing wrong with that. A paycheck from a corporate or retail job clears the same and has the same functionality: to pay your bills. No judgment.

However, if you are able to start the journey of finding ful-filling work or a job that you like, then here is how and why you should do it. That job you hate that's stressing you out? Yeah, not to be dramatic, but it's slowly killing you. Poor stress man-agement is the number one cause of deadly cardiovascular diseases in Black women. Sooo, getting a job that doesn't send your body into toxic stress can literally save your life.

One way to begin this journey is by spending time with yourself to figure out what you value most in a career. Then, make a list of things you genuinely enjoy and see if you can find a work field that aligns with these elements.

Take Action

Does your job bring you joy? If not, think about what is holding you back from looking for a new place to work.

Develop Your Version
of a Balanced Life

" *I think you have to be comfortable with perhaps not being perfect at [both work and parenting] all the time.* "

KETANJI BROWN JACKSON, Associate Justice of the
Supreme Court of the United States, in a 2022
interview with *The Washington Post*

MEDITATION

It is okay for my life to be a bit messy.

REFLECTION

Not to burst your bubble, but the idea of work-life balance is a myth. When it comes to balancing your life, there's always talk of mainly balancing work and home life. For mothers, this includes parenting. However, your life is not split into just two areas of care and existence. You're not just at work and then home being a caregiver. You're out and about in the world with other parts of you that deserve to be nurtured, like your mental health and social life.

You're probably thinking: If having a work-life balance is not a real thing, then what is the other option? An imperfect life that is a little bit messy. Seriously. Now, *you* get to define your version of imperfect and messy. Our girl, Ketanji Brown Jackson, is correct in her quote: You are not always gonna get it right at home or at work, so you have to get comfortable with being imperfect. And that applies to any other area of your life. If you find the idea of embracing being imperfect uncomfortable, let's talk further about it.

For you as a Black woman, allowing yourself to let go of perfectionism is likely hard. Your identity and your anxiety may be wrapped up in it. It doesn't serve you to be seen by your spouse, children, friends, coworkers, etc., as someone who is always put together. It commodifies you. Because when you have real-life moments where you come undone, you want to be seen as human. Don't participate in our oppressors' ideology of dehumanizing us—which, in this case, is disguised as perfectionism. I digress.

Nonetheless, to develop your version of a balanced life, you will have to identify the areas in your life you want to pour your energy into. Then, work through understanding that you may not get it right all the time. And that's okay.

Take Action

Take time to explore what your version of a balanced life would look like. What would your daily routines be?

Let Go of Fear

NINA SIMONE, singer, civil rights activist,
in *Nina: An Historical Perspective* in 1970

MEDITATION

I will not allow my fears to hold me back from achieving my goals.

REFLECTION

Fear can leave the mind, body, and soul paralyzed. It will hold you back from achieving your goals and creating the life of your dreams. Most fears start in the mind and make a home inside of you. Trapped with nowhere to go, this may cause you to internalize the lies of your fears. You need to tell those worries of yours to find another place to live. They've officially been evicted.

The kind of fears being considered in this reflection are not those tied to things like phobias and other mental health conditions. Instead, they are the thoughts and associated feelings rooted in the perception you have of yourself. Thoughts like, *I can't do that because I'm not...* or, *I shouldn't do that because I'm not...*

For the most part, many fears are based on lived experiences—especially as a Black woman. From a young age, the world and community around you try to convince you that there is a limit to all that you can accomplish. Whether it was the judgment you received from caregivers and teachers, or the lack of identity representation in positions of power and influence, being fearful of your greatest capabilities was instilled in you.

When you're unable to move past these fearful thoughts, it usually means you lack self-trust. Trust that you can handle whatever emotional stings you may experience because of the obstacles that stand between you and your desires. Let go of your fears and embrace trusting yourself. It will lead you to a path of true freedom—freedom from what other people think and freedom to live your life according to your own plan.

Take Action

Ask yourself the following question:
What fears are holding me back from achieving my goals? Write 'em down.

Let Your Light Shine

" Don't try to lessen yourself for the world; let the world catch up to you. "

BEYONCÉ, singer, songwriter, businesswoman

MEDITATION

I will not allow the world to dim my light.

REFLECTION

As a Black woman, it is important that you never dim your light for anyone. This means that you don't shrink yourself in rooms you're in to appease anybody else's comfortability with your presence. The truth is, society will always try to dictate how you should show up in different spaces, adhere to stereotypes, or downplay your accomplishments. You do not have to buckle to these pressures to be accepted. Embrace who you are. Let the world see you shine brightly as you defy the limitations that others try to impose on you.

Do not be afraid to take up space, sis. Walking a path that is lit up by your authenticity and confidence will always be rewarding. You will not only feel empowered to boldly pursue your dreams, but you will also encourage other people to do the same. That's why many will try to get you to lessen yourself for the world. Your light is a threat to a society that is deter-mined to lift up negativity. Remember, someone who is unapol-ogetically themselves is a powerful person because they are not afraid to create change and break barriers.

Learning to not dim your light will take practice. First, you will have to acknowledge your feelings, exploring what scares you about boldly presenting yourself to the world. Next, work on building your self-confidence by doing things like setting attainable goals and celebrating your successes. Most impor-tantly, challenge those negative thoughts of yours by engaging in positive self-talk to continue to build your self-assuredness. Lastly, focus on the people in your life who accept and love you; shine bright for them and embrace their support.

Take Action

Explore your feelings. How does it feel when you are free to be yourself?

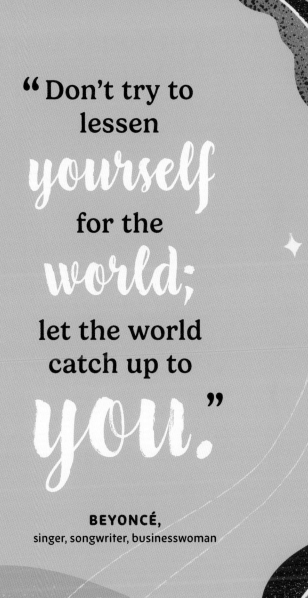

"Don't try to lessen yourself for the world; let the world catch up to you."

BEYONCÉ,
singer, songwriter, businesswoman

Accept Your Current Journey

66 *Sometimes, what you're looking for is already there.* 99

ARETHA FRANKLIN, singer

MEDITATION

Accepting my life brings me peace.

REFLECTION

Learning to accept your current life's journey will help you manage your mental health. Focusing on the future or the past will only do one thing: increase your anxiety. When you're too focused on your past, future, or other people's lives, you're not paying attention to yourself. This causes you to be distracted instead of staying focused on your own goals. This is why you must practice being present with yourself. To do that, start by taking note of your life at this moment and think about what you are grateful for. Breathe in acceptance and breathe out peace.

Now, if you're a high-achieving Black woman (like me!), you might find this hard to do. That's because you're always focused on your next achievement, next degree, etc. Sis, slow down. Practicing acceptance releases you from any internal and external pressure to do it all. Additionally, sometimes we can be so focused on our future endeavors that we don't take a moment to enjoy our current blessings and successes. You know...the ones you probably prayed for? Yeah, those.

In addition, we live in a society that thrives off of hustle culture—the concept that you must always be doing more to make more money or secure the bag. Subscribing to this rise-and-grind mentality is stressful. It will have you thinking that you need to *do the most* to find happiness or grab your next life-changing opportunity. But that's not true. You don't have to search far and wide to find the peace and happiness you need. It lives right within you and just needs to be accessed by you.

Take Action

Take time to think about the following: Do you struggle with accepting your current life's journey? If so, why?

Break Generational Trauma Patterns

" Your body will remember your generational trauma, but it will also remember your generational healing. "

DR. MARIEL BUQUÉ, psychologist, author of *Break the Cycle: A Guide to Healing Intergenerational Trauma*

MEDITATION

Breaking generational trauma patterns requires me to embrace the healing process.

REFLECTION

It's tough work breaking generational trauma patterns (a.k.a. generational curses). However, it is something you must attempt on your wellness journey. Generational trauma patterns, such as poor conflict resolution skills, are traumas passed down from the previous generation. Intergenerational trauma can be passed down from parents, grandparents, and the collective Black community. While you work on breaking these familial trauma patterns, you can also embrace the healing that will be done through you for the generations around you. The focus doesn't always have to be on the hard habit-changing work you're doing.

You have to make the decision that unhealthy generational patterns stop with you. When you heal, everybody around you now has permission to do the same. If you don't do the work to heal from toxic generational cycles, the trauma will live inside of you. This can add unnecessary stress to your mind, body, and soul.

To begin or continue the work of breaking intergenerational trauma, you must first remember to be kind and gentle with yourself. This kind of healing will ask a lot of you, so pace yourself. With healing trauma, another thing that must be done upfront is establishing safety: safety within yourself, with others, and in your environment. Be sure to connect with people you trust (like your bestie) as you engage in generational healing work. If needed, get in touch with a mental health professional so they can accompany you on your healing journey, as some things that come up may be hard to process. Most importantly, let the healing process guide you back to yourself as you strip away the layers of trauma that have encapsulated you.

Take Action

Answer the question: In what ways do you feel like you are breaking generational trauma patterns?

Give Yourself Permission to Live

❝ So, if my life is actually mine...then I have to really live it for myself. I have to put myself first and not be looking for permission to do so. ❞

TRACEE ELLIS ROSS, actor, in her speech at *Glamour*'s 2017 Women of the Year Summit

MEDITATION

I give myself permission to live my life according to my own plans.

REFLECTION

If you truly want to live a stress-free life, you are going to have to stop caring about what other people think of your life choices. This means giving yourself permission to live according to your own plans. Not your mama's, your daddy's, or whoever's. *Just yours.* Sounds exciting, doesn't it?

Now, of course, this is easier said than done, but it must be done! Yes, it is hard trying to live a life that goes against the expectations of family, friends, and society, especially as a Black woman, as it feels like everybody has an opinion on what your life should look like. But they're not you, so their thoughts do not matter. Only you know how you want to live your best life.

To start living your best life, you must first get to know yourself. Spend some alone time with yourself, doing activities that you like or have never tried before. You will need to go on a self-discovery journey to really understand yourself better. Once you do this, you'll be able to decide what your future looks like. Is it filled with marriage, vacations, kids, business ventures, etc.? Only you can decide that.

So, be grateful, beloved. Now more than ever, we have the privilege to live a life that is truly ours. Black women's lives are no longer dictated by things like the men they marry. We now have the freedom to be truly independent and build the beautiful lives of our dreams. Really think about it. How would you want to spend the rest of your years on Earth? Go after that life. It's waiting for you. Give yourself permission to live.

Take Action

Spend some time thinking about ways you can live according to your own plans.

Find Your Alignment

66 *When the heart is right, the mind and the body will follow.* **99**

CORETTA SCOTT KING, author, activist, civil rights leader

MEDITATION

Finding my alignment in life is a journey, not a destination.

REFLECTION

Making sure that your life is aligned with who you are as a person is important to your self-care journey. It will help you maintain the health of your mind, body, and soul. Being in alignment means not only staying true to who you are as a person but also positively embracing your life's intricate path. The truth is, finding and staying in alignment with your inner self is a journey, not a destination. It's an exercise in making sure that you are tapped into who you are on a daily basis.

To find the things that align with your truest self, you have to make space to get to know yourself. This can look like moving away from your hometown, trying a new hobby, making decisions without anybody's input, or spending quality time with yourself to simply reflect on your life (*cough* like with this book *cough*). The reason you need to be intentional about getting to know yourself is that, often as we grow up, Black women are influenced by the traumas of our lived experiences. You can lose yourself in the shuffle of life, trying to conform to how your surrounding community and society tell you to think and behave.

So girl, it's time to shake off any standards that the world has imposed on you that have hindered you from connecting with yourself. Be proactive about staying in alignment with your life's path. The more you do it, the better you will feel. You will find that many aspects of your life will improve, such as your relationships, work life, and overall health. Once you find your-self, everything else will fall in line.

Take Action

Ask yourself: *Does my life reflect my truest desires?*
If not, brainstorm ways to get yourself one step closer
to feeling aligned in all parts of your life.

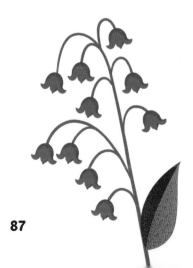

Ignore Others' Limited Beliefs

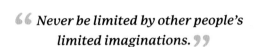

Never be limited by other people's limited imaginations.

DR. MAE CAROL JEMISON, American engineer, physician, former NASA astronaut

MEDITATION

My thoughts and beliefs do not require anybody else's validation.

REFLECTION

The world will always try to convince you that you are unable to accomplish more than you think. Forget that. Refusing to let people talk you out of your hopes and dreams is the ultimate cheat code. It's your life. You should have the primary influence over it. One of the worst feelings is having a big idea, telling someone about it, and them speaking doubt over it. Like, please. Hush up. Now you're questioning yourself and swaying away from your truest desires, disconnected from your inner self. If you find that you are easily swayed by other people's thoughts and beliefs about your life decisions, then it's time to work on having your voice be the loudest and most encouraging one in your head.

Additionally, letting your imagination run wild and create different possibilities for the outcome of your life and goals is beneficial to your mental well-being. When you stop yourself from dreaming and thinking broadly about the things you can accomplish, you adopt a scarcity mindset—you know, the belief that you only have access to limited resources. Instead, you should lean into an abundant mindset, the belief that, no matter your current circumstances, you can access the world's unlimited resources. Now, will you get them immediately? Probably not. But you can take steps toward obtaining these unlimited resources by not allowing your mind to be limited by other people's limited beliefs.

To stop other people's limited thinking from impacting your thoughts and beliefs, you must first let go of the need for validation from others. Your desire to reach a goal or complete a task is valid enough. Also, choose safe people to share your wildest dreams with—people who you know will uplift and support you. Lastly, if you ever feel doubt creep into your mind because of something someone said, challenge it immediately with a positive affirmation or thought like, *The things I desire are within my reach.*

Take Action

Explore whether there are any limiting beliefs, influenced by external situations, that are holding you back from pursuing your wildest dreams.

Get Real with Your Growth

❝ *Your willingness to look at your darkness is what empowers you to change.* ❞

IYANLA VANZANT, author, spiritual teacher, life coach

MEDITATION

The discomfort I feel from change is necessary for my personal growth.

REFLECTION

Okay, girl. It's time to get real about your personal growth journey. This means being completely honest with yourself about how you show up for yourself, in relationships, at work, etc. A lot of times, as Black women, we build up a defense wall around our inner selves to protect us from all the previous harm we may have experienced—which, honestly, is an appropriate response, because you might feel like there's no way you are going to allow someone or something to play in your face again. As a result, you might have some troubling behaviors. For example, you might treat people harshly or with judgment or feel like you must do everything yourself because you lack trust in others. This creates more stress cycles for yourself.

Let's address your emotional wounds and toxic behaviors, so that you can ease into positive change.

The fact is, change is hard work. It's self-care, and self-care is not always things like long walks and deep tissue massages. Sometimes, it's looking at our not-so-nice traits and thinking about how we can transform them so they do not disrupt our daily lives, especially our different relationships. To enhance your personal growth journey, you'll have to make space to evaluate the parts of yourself that you may not like. The best place to start is by thinking about the things that make you insecure and go from there. Getting real about the areas of your life that need growth is one of the many first steps to powerful change. It will get uncomfortable, but on the other side of that discomfort is more peace and better self-esteem.

Take Action

Get real with where you are on your personal growth journey. Are you good? Or is there something you could work on? Think about it.

Benefit from Your Resilience

> ❝ *I'm convinced that we Black women possess a special indestructible strength that allows us to not only get down, but to get up, to get through, and to get over.* ❞

JANET JACKSON, singer, songwriter, actor, dancer,
in her speech at the Soul Train Awards in 2004

MEDITATION

Only I get to decide when I need to be resilient.

REFLECTION

Take your cape off. Being a "strong Black woman" is worn out. But being able to pick yourself up *when you're ready* and continue moving through life after dealing with hardships is not. That's called having resilience—the ability to cope, adapt, and thrive after a crisis. When used appropriately, it's a very powerful psychological tool. It's what keeps you on track toward your goals.

As a collective, we Black women are in our self-care era, especially you reading this book. We are putting ourselves first like it's nobody's business (*'cause it's not*). Every day, we may face situations that pressure us to withstand emotional suffering silently. Historically, that is what society has asked of us: stand-up and be strong for the world while ignoring our needs. As a result, we have decided that enough is enough. Soft life vibes only.

However, it's important to remember that you can be soft and strong. Do not relinquish your inner strength to spite the world's burdens that are unfairly placed on you. It is okay to recognize that you have resilience and are a powerful person because of it. What matters is what is influencing you to tap into your inner resilience. Is it your anxiety? Your fear of being rejected or abandoned? Or could it be your need to prove your worth to yourself or others? *Oop.* Just some things to think about.

All in all, having resilience is not about being a "strong Black woman." It's about knowing your worth and wielding that power whenever you desire.

Take Action

Take a moment to tell yourself how proud you are of yourself for having enough resilience to make it through your last tough situation.

" I'm convinced
that we Black women
possess a special
indestructible

strength

that allows us to
not only get down,
but to get up,
to get through,
and to get over. "

JANET JACKSON,
singer, songwriter, actor, dancer,
in her speech at the Soul Train Awards in 2004

Put Yourself First

*❝ If you prioritize yourself,
you are going to save yourself. ❞*

GABRIELLE UNION, actor, author, in *We're Going to Need More
Wine: Stories That Are Funny, Complicated and True*

MEDITATION

Choosing to put myself first is
how I reclaim my life.

REFLECTION

Reminder: You can't help others if you don't take care of yourself first. (Read the Prioritize Your Self-Care meditation earlier
in this book.) Prioritizing your needs can be a matter of life and
death. Literally. Your needs are things that help you to move
through life with peace and comfort. If you're not putting yourself first and receiving the things you require to thrive, you risk
deteriorating your mental and physical health. However, sometimes as Black women, we find it hard to make ourselves a pri-
ority and get or ask for what we desire. We get too caught up
in our roles at home, at work, or in our community. After all, the
world does send us messages that our lives do not matter and
our value is found in positions of supporting others, which is

wrong. You are so deserving of being taken care of and having your needs met—especially by you.

Choosing to put yourself first is an act of self-preservation. It's how you take back your life and reconnect with yourself. Learning how to better prioritize your needs is a great step in that direction. To do that, you need to first figure out what you need in different areas of your life: home, work, relationships, and health are great places to start. Now, this list may change over your lifetime, but that's okay. It's about being in touch with yourself to know what will provide you with the care you are seeking. Lastly, you need to develop the strength to either go get your needs by yourself or ask others for help. It is okay to have needs in all areas of your life, especially your relation-ships. You may feel like, *oh I don't need anybody; I got it*, which is okay as you should know how you can meet your own needs, but it's also okay to ask the people in your life to give you what you require. And if they can't, then that's okay. You just need the courage to ask because you and your needs matter.

Take Action

Think about it: What are some ways you can make sure that you are having your needs met every day?

Hold Space for Accountability

IDA B. WELLS, journalist, educator, civil rights leader, in *The
Light of Truth: Writings of an Anti-Lynching Crusader*

MEDITATION

**Holding myself and others accountable
for our actions is an act of healing.**

REFLECTION

Learning to take accountability for your actions is one of the best things you can do for your mental well-being. The ability to take responsibility for the impact your thoughts, feelings, and behaviors have on you and others gives *I am healing* energy. Additionally, you must also get comfortable holding others responsible for the impact their wrongdoing has on you and the community. Accountability shines a light on the things that are wrong so that things can be changed for the better. It helps you to get real about your personal healing journey.

Holding yourself responsible for your own well-being requires increasing your self-awareness by being super honest with yourself. Sometimes, as a Black woman, you will find yourself caught up in the hustle and bustle of the world, trying to thrive and survive, and, as a result, you may become numb to emotions and disconnect from yourself. When we are disconnected from ourselves, we are not aware of things we do that might be harming others. This is why you need to make space for accountability—to reconnect with your inner self. Also, if you've ever experienced the pains of microaggressions and misogynoir, you know how hard it can be to get someone to be aware of the damage they've done to you. While not everyone who does you wrong will recognize their mistake, you must attempt to shine a light on this issue at the moment you experience it. Don't be afraid to speak your truth. And if you need more encouragement on why you should speak your truth, re-read the Get Real with Your Growth meditation.

Take Action

Do you need to get honest with yourself or others about something? Think about it.

Heal Through Community

MEDITATION

My community is a powerful tool for my healing journey.

REFLECTION

Nothing beats a safe space for Black women like Black women. When it comes to your wellness journey, please know that you do not have to do it alone. You can find solace in healing through your community. Your community can include friends, family, people going through similar circumstances, and other trusted individuals. These are folks who, when you're feeling crappy about your personal growth journey, will fill you up with self-confidence and not self-doubt.

Using community as a form of self-care is something that Black women have been doing for centuries all over the world. Because one thing our people will do is *make it do what it do,* even with a lack of resources thanks to good ol' systemic racism. Gatherings, whether they be in community centers, a neighbor's home, or places like churches, have always been an integral part of healing the Black collective—with Black women at the head of it. There's nothing a barbecue with "Summertime" blasting in the background can't fix.

Ultimately, healing through community is important because of one aspect: co-regulation. This is the ability to emotionally regulate and cope with the help of other individuals. When we heal ourselves and gather with others who bring us joy and a sense of community, we take better care of ourselves and each other. If you're having a hard time finding people you can rock with, start by doing an activity you love. Finding others who have similar interests is a great place to start building a strong foundation for a community.

Take Action

Identify safe people in your life (loved ones you trust) who can help you on your wellness journey.

Trust Your Intuition

> **Happiness comes from living as you need to, as you want to. As your inner voice tells you to. Happiness comes from being who you actually are instead of who you think you are supposed to be.**

SHONDA RHIMES, television producer, screenwriter, author, in *Year of Yes: How to Dance It Out, Stand In the Sun and Be Your Own Person*

MEDITATION

Listening to my intuition will lead me to my happiness.

REFLECTION

Not listening to your intuition will always have consequences—good or bad. Your intuition is the guiding light within you that leads you to make life decisions that align with your happiness. Not trusting your inner voice will leave you with feelings of self-betrayal. As a Black woman, you are probably all too familiar with self-betrayal. You were most likely conditioned from a young age to ignore your intuition and instructed through societal messages to conform to the dominant culture (ahem, white supremacy), even if it wasn't true to who you were as a person.

As a result, self-betrayal became a means of survival against microaggressions, racism, and sexism. Let's shake off the need to ignore your intuition and lean into listening to and trusting it.

To get better at trusting your intuition, you'll first have to learn what that voice feels like, because sometimes your intuition and your anxiety can get their wires crossed. Then, you're left not knowing which inner thoughts to listen to for guidance. But girl, pro tip: Thoughts tied to your intuition are usually more calming, while anxious thoughts feel chaotic. Once you've identified what your intuition sounds or feels like, you'll have to do little things to help build up your confidence to trust yourself. For example, making decisions without consulting anyone else. This will help create self-trust because getting used to that uncomfortable feeling of *Will this work out?* when you make a life decision is part of the process of trusting your intuition. Embrace it. Your happiness awaits you.

Take Action

Think about the last time you ignored your intuition. Reflect on how that felt.

Pursue Your Passions Boldly

66 *Now is not the time to be silent. Find your purpose,
pursue it relentlessly, passionately, and loudly.* 99

ANGELA BASSETT, actor, at the Black Girls Rock Awards 2019

MEDITATION

It is okay for me to be loud about my passions.

REFLECTION

You only have one life to live, sis. Stop playing games. You must pursue your passions boldly and with purpose. No more shrinking yourself. If you're more of the move-in-silence-as-you-chase-your-dreams type, that's okay. You can still be relentless in your pursuit of those dreams. In a world where Black women face systemic and individual obstacles to achieve our goals, finding your purpose through your passion is helpful in providing the guidance to go around the hurdles.

Finding your purpose and passion is essential to maintaining your overall wellness. It will give you a sense of belonging, a spiritual connection to the world, and help you feel better by improving your self-esteem. Additionally, it will be the battery pack in your back as you go through the different stages of life. To find your purpose, you need to figure out what you're passionate about. Your passions are things that bring you joy and make you feel like you're contributing to society's greater good. For example, *ya girl* who wrote this book is passionate about encouraging Black women to practice self-care and prioritize their wellness needs. As a result, writing skills were used to help further that passion, giving me a greater sense of purpose. It is time for you to step out of your comfort zone and pursue your passions boldly.

Take Action

Take a moment to think about the things you are passionate about. Are you pursuing them? If not, how come? If yes, how so?

Give Yourself the Space to Grow

MEDITATION

I am allowed space and grace
to grow as a person.

REFLECTION

Sometimes, we want to rush our healing and our personal growth. But the truth is, you need time when dealing with traumas and new skills. It takes just as much time to heal from our pain as it took to endure it, and there is a learning curve when developing new life or coping skills. Like the quote mentioned in this meditation, give yourself permission to write...rewrite... unwrite...your life's story.

As Black women, we often find it hard to extend ourselves the same grace we give others. We are expected to be kind and keep our mouths shut about the horrible things that are done to us at home, work, school, etc., and move forward. But, girl, if you have endured years of mistreatment and negative conditioning about your existence in society, you have a lot of unlearning and relearning to do. Your brain and body have the capacity to do it and just need space and grace.

Being able to give yourself these things is re-humanizing your lived experiences. The dehumanization that Black women go through on a regular basis is at the core of a lot of our troubles. We need to learn to treat ourselves as the delicate human beings we are, and providing yourself with enough room to grow is a great way to do that. There is no need to rush your healing or learning. Trust the timeline of your life and keep it pushing. You are allowed to have space and grace to grow as a person.

Take Action

Be honest with yourself and explore how much space and grace you actually give yourself when completing tasks.

Take Up Space

❝ If they don't give you a seat at the table, bring a folding chair. ❞

SHIRLEY CHISHOLM, first Black woman to be
elected to the United States Congress

MEDITATION

I am not afraid to take up space in
rooms I feel I deserve to be in.

REFLECTION

Learning to take up space in every place you occupy is important to your wellness journey. For centuries, Black women have
been told that we do not have any power against the dominant
culture (a.k.a. white supremacy). Obviously, history says other-
wise. Black women have constantly been among the changemakers (like Shirley Chisholm) who shift the culture in a better
direction for the people.

But the thing is, power hoarding is an element of white
supremacy culture. It is damaging to all marginalized communities because it tries to make us believe that power is not in
abundance. We must either fight to get it, keep other community members away from it, or never attempt to get it. *Wrong.*

You have every right to be part of the spaces that are making decisions that impact your life. Spaces like your home, work, school, or your community.

Taking up space means you boldly show up as your full self in whatever rooms you occupy. No longer do you need to shrink your presence. You deserve to be seen and heard. As a Black woman, you will be hypervisible *and* invisible at the same time. Being hypervisible means that you will be othered, watched, and judged. You might be the only Black person in the room, so everybody sees you. Being invisible means that some folks will ignore you because, to them, your lived experience is not one of value. You might find yourself shut out of better opportunities for success, also known as "the table." So, if you're not invited to the table, create your own or pull up to it and take up space.

Take Action

Consider the following: What areas of your life are calling you to take up more space?

" If they don't give you a

seat

at the

table,

bring a
folding chair. "

SHIRLEY CHISHOLM,
first Black woman to be elected to
the United States Congress

Navigate the Unexpected with Courage

> **" Storms happen. Storms are natural. It's all about how you weather them. It's all about how you navigate through them, but you will make it through the storm. You have before and you always will. Just put on your raincoat, baby! "**

ISSA RAE, actor, writer, producer, to *People* at the 2024 American Black Film Festival

MEDITATION

I am confident in my ability to navigate the unexpected.

REFLECTION

Think about the last time you went through some hard stuff. Did it break you, build you, or both? It's okay if it was somewhere in between or all the above. Let's be real: Sometimes, we go through things that are straight-up traumatizing, and the only appropriate response is to have a meltdown and get the support we need. However, no matter your response and recovery, you still made it through. You were able to navigate the unexpected. The unexpected is any situation that you didn't see coming, and now you must quickly adapt. Thankfully, as Black women, that is one of our superpowers.

To be able to deal with troubling circumstances when they pop out of nowhere, you must increase your self-confidence. When you are sure about yourself, you trust that you have the capacity to know how to handle stressful unforeseen situations. So, remember to take a breather as soon as you're met with the unexpected and challenge any negative thoughts about your capabilities. Then, go into problem-solving mode, remembering that there are always solutions and options to managing your issues. You don't have to do it alone, but if you do, you *can* handle it. When all is said and done, you can put on your white coat, seek out the support you need to manage your problem, and say, "It's handled," Ms. Olivia Pope style (and watch her handle all manner of problems in *Scandal*).

Take Action

If you're going through a hard time, remind yourself of your ability to navigate the unexpected. And if you aren't going through a hard time, reflect on a past unexpected situation that you handled well.

Speak Your Truth

> 66 *I believe that telling our stories, first to ourselves and then to one another and the world, is a revolutionary act.* 99

JANET MOCK, writer, television producer, transgender rights activist, in *Redefining Realness: My Path to Womanhood, Identity, Love & So Much More*

MEDITATION

Speaking my truth will always bring me more peace.

REFLECTION

Never be afraid to speak your truth about the things you experience in this world as a Black woman. It is, in fact, a revolutionary act for you to share the things you go through, first with yourself and then with the people around you. This is because the world we live in asks us to hush our mouths and be quiet: the truth about the things we go through as Black women in this society are dehumanizing. Nobody expects you to speak up for yourself. They want you to remain silent, but speaking your truth about whatever it is, whether it be microaggressions, racism, sexism, ageism, etc., helps you to reclaim your voice.

It's important that you speak your truth to yourself first, which means being honest with yourself about the things you've been through. Sometimes, we must tell our stories to ourselves first so that we can process it and then be able to share it. This is how you live authentically, and living authentically is beneficial for your well-being. If you find it hard to say what's on your chest, then you need to start small and safe. Share your lived experiences with people you trust who will give you validation and feedback, if desired. You need to be able to use your voice as a Black woman. Only you have the power to tell your story. Sharing your story with others is how you build community, and community is an integral part of any wellness journey.

Take Action

What's something you've been eager to get off your chest regarding your experiences as a Black woman? Share it with someone you trust.

Customize Your Life's Journey

> **If you have no road map, you have to create your own.**

JACQUELINE WOODSON, author, *Los Angeles Times* Festival of Books 2015

MEDITATION

I must be the pioneer of my own life.

REFLECTION

Are you waiting for someone to come along and help you figure out what you should do with your life? If this sounds like you, then it's time for you to get up. You are the one in charge of your life. The keys to your life's journey are in your hands; grab 'em.

Figuring out what you want to do in this world is one of life's greatest gifts and obstacles. If it's not systemic roadblocks like wage gap or racism, it's a lack of self-efficacy due to internalized negative societal messaging about Black women. Often, we are the first ones in many of the rooms we enter, doing things that perhaps our family or anyone who looks like us has never done before. Not having an example of how something can be done by kinfolk is overwhelming and a huge undertaking. You're put in a position to create your own road map, and that's okay. Do not be discouraged. This is an opportunity that you must embrace, because there isn't just one path to your goal's destination.

To be the pioneer in your own life, do the necessary research and get comfortable with riding solo. You will find yourself alone on your journey for a long time at first. But what's remarkable is that, on your way to your goal, you can pick up others along the way. That means creating a community for yourself. Yes, you are creating your own path, but it's more fun with others on it. Having the guts to customize your life's journey will help you to increase your self-esteem, build boundaries, and open your life to many adventures. So, get to it, girl. You got this.

Take Action

If you're feeling stuck about some life decisions, ask yourself: *Am I waiting for someone else to map out the path for me?*

Activate Your Grief

66 *May we not just grieve, but give.*
***May we not just ache, but act.* 99**

AMANDA GORMAN, poet, activist, in *Hymn for the Hurting*

MEDITATION

I don't have to sit in my grief; it can
activate me for a purpose.

REFLECTION

Experiencing a loss of any kind is devastating. Whether it's a
person, place, or thing, having to grieve something you have
lost permanently is tough. It takes your breath away, leaving
you depressed and in disbelief. While there are five common
stages of grief—denial, anger, bargaining, depression, and
acceptance—they are often not experienced in any specific
order. You may find yourself wavering between all the stages
for months or years, only to one day wake up and feel a sense
of peace with your grief. There's no getting over a loss, especially if it's a death. You just learn to move forward without
having your grief completely disrupt your life.

When you feel the time is right, you are allowed to channel your grief into something greater. For example, in the Black

community we experience death on both a personal and collective level. Every time a Black person is fatally harmed by law enforcement or a racist individual (#SayHerName), you feel that pain because you think about how that could've been you, a family member, or someone you know. It's scary, so you take that pain and rage and channel it into a social justice movement or the act of simply checking in on your friends or community.

Ultimately, there is no perfect way to manage grief and loss. However, it's important that you stay in tune with how you are feeling, tending to your emotions with gentle care. Let others around you know what you need, even if you don't know what that is exactly. Stay in community with a mental health professional or other loved ones, as you are not alone in the grief you are processing, and you don't have to go at it alone.

Take Action

Reflect on some ways that you can be gentle with yourself when you experience grief and loss.

Lean Into Self-Respect

> ❝ *I must undertake to love myself and to respect myself as though my very life depends upon self-love and self-respect.* ❞

JUNE JORDAN, poet, essayist, teacher, activist, in *Civil Wars*

MEDITATION

If I don't love and respect myself first, nobody else will.

REFLECTION

Like Malcolm X once said, "The most disrespected person in America is the Black woman. The most unprotected person in America is the Black woman. The most neglected person in America is the Black woman." Thus, good sis, you must lean into respecting your own darn self because the world will manipulate you into thinking that the disrespect you often experience is in your head. FYI: it's not.

To lean into self-respect, you've got to develop self-confidence, which starts with learning to accept yourself, including your personality traits and interests. You must love who you are as a person from the inside out because the world will try to trick you into thinking that you are unlovable.

Furthermore, to build up your self-respect, you'll have to know and enforce your boundaries, have compassion for yourself, take responsibility for your actions and choices, honor your values, surround yourself with people who care about you, and become assertive. Whew. That's a lot, but these are all things that you can slowly practice.

Leading every day with self-respect is a journey as a Black woman. It can look like the following: not allowing others to touch your hair, making sure people say your name correctly, and avoiding or addressing microaggressions in the moment. It's not your job to make non-Black folks feel comfortable around you, but it is your job to make sure your actions reflect the respect you have for yourself.

Take Action

Be honest with yourself and think about this:
Are your thoughts and actions filled with self-love and self-respect?

Leave Spaces That Don't Serve You

66 *I don't want to force myself into an institution that doesn't seem to appreciate what I bring.* 99

NIKOLE HANNAH JONES, journalist, author, to CNN's *New Day* in 2021

MEDITATION

My presence is not required in spaces that actively reject me.

REFLECTION

Never be afraid to leave environments that cause you stress and make you feel othered. Often, many of us desire to have a "seat at the table" because Black women are often excluded from spaces that provide greater opportunities for success. But, uh, you don't need a "seat at the table." As a matter of fact, you're allowed to walk past that table, pretend it never existed, and create your own.

In the work environment, Black women often experience being the pet to the threat. The corporate girlies know exactly what that is. You were hired because of your skill and the diversity you bring to the workspace. Then, you become exceptional at your job. Everybody loves you—or so you think. Then suddenly, colleagues begin to make life hard for you. You're left off projects, asked to take on a bigger workload, overly criticized, and highly surveilled. Someone at your job is waiting for you to mess up so they can have a reason to fire you. It's exhausting. Your job becomes your primary source of stress, and you have no choice but to leave for the sake of your health. It sucks. However, what is worse is staying at a place that no longer serves you peace and love.

Take Action

Are there any environments you frequent that are currently causing you stress and making you feel othered? Start plotting your exit.

Hold On to Hope

❝ Don't ever make decisions based on fear. Make decisions based on hope and possibility. Make decisions based on what should happen, not what shouldn't. ❞

MICHELLE OBAMA, former First Lady of the United States

MEDITATION

I will not be led by my fears but by my hopes.

REFLECTION

Like with many things, Michelle Obama, former First Lady of the United States, is right about this: Making decisions in your life will require you to lean into hope and not fear. This is because hope is the driving force that keeps you moving forward whenever you have to deal with adversity.

Now, holding onto hope is easier said than done. You move through this world as a member of a marginalized group and are unfortunately more likely to experience things that may make you question if hope even exists. When misogynoir rears its ugly head your way through someone's word or actions, it can be hurtful. As a result, you may put up emotional walls and lean into an anxious mindset, making decisions out of fear and self-protection. However, you cannot succumb to your anxious thoughts.

To lean into hope, you will have to acknowledge your feelings. If you're feeling anxious, breathe deeply and release your fears around whatever stressful circumstances you're currently dealing with. Inhale, *I will be led by my hopes*, and exhale, *I will not be led by my fears*. Next, you will have to process your thoughts. This can be done verbally with a trusted loved one or mental health professional. Or, you can write out your feelings in a journal. Either way, if you struggle with holding onto hope when needing to make tough life decisions, slow down and then proceed.

Take Action

Explore any recent decisions you've made. Did you make those decisions out of fear or hope?

"Don't ever make decisions based on fear. Make decisions based on

hope and possibility.

Make decisions based on what should happen, not what shouldn't."

MICHELLE OBAMA,
former First Lady of the United States

Define Your Identity

" Defining myself, as opposed to being defined by others, is one of the most difficult challenges I face. "

CAROL MOSELEY-BRAUN, politician, lawyer

MEDITATION

Only I have the power to define my identity as a Black woman.

REFLECTION

Black women are not a monolith. While we share the same identity, each of us has a story that is unique to our lived experiences. However, the hypervisibility of being a Black woman means that everybody and their mama believes they have a say in how you should show up in this world because of your race and gender. As a result, you'll have to learn to tune out the white noise (pun intended) and define your Black womanhood for yourself.

There will come a time when you have a reckoning with your intersecting identities. You will have to decide if your life decisions will be influenced by negative stereotypes or by your own definition of being a Black woman. Whichever way you choose to present yourself to the world is valid. Your Blackness and womanhood are not commodities that can be revoked based on your behavior. (Unless you don't know the "Electric Slide!") If you present to the world as a Black woman, you are a Black woman.

Ultimately, building a strong relationship with your identity will help you not internalize racist and sexist ideologies about Black women. When you're assured about who you are, the lies of misogynoir do not attach to your self-image or how you view yourself. The way you choose to move through this world defines who you are as a person, not the collective sisterhood of Black women. Only you can define who you are as a person, as you are not responsible for how others perceive your identity.

Take Action

Take time to think about your relationship with your identity as a Black woman. Do you love it, or do you love it?

Make Time to Understand Yourself

66 *If you don't understand yourself, you don't understand anybody else.* **99**

NIKKI GIOVANNI, poet, writer, activist, educator, in conversation with James Baldwin on *SOUL!* in 1971

MEDITATION

My most important relationship is the one I have with myself.

REFLECTION

Understanding yourself opens doors to understanding others because we are all here on Earth having a shared human experience. It's vital that as a Black woman, you learn to humanize your lived experiences. The dehumanizing experience of micro-aggressions and misogynoir can have a lasting impact on you, causing you to disconnect or dissociate from yourself. Now, this is something you don't want to do, as it leads to self-betrayal and misalignment with your true self. Thus, you must make time to better understand yourself. The most important relationship that you have is with yourself. It influences everything about your life, especially your relationships.

To get to know yourself better, you must make time for it. This can look like spending time in nature, meditating (ahem, with this book perhaps?), and having quiet time to think and explore your thoughts and feelings. Another way to get to know yourself is to explore new hobbies and activities. The time you spend understanding yourself will help you to have a better relationship with yourself. Additionally, having a better understanding of who you are will not happen overnight. There is no perfect timeline to a stronger relationship with yourself. What matters is that you continue to pour into yourself first on your journey of self-discovery. You can't pour into others from an empty cup. Get serious about getting to know yourself.

Take Action

What is your relationship like with yourself? Do you feel like you have a good understanding of yourself? Think about it.

Free Yourself from Negative Influences

66 *Whatever is bringing you down, get rid of it. Because you'll find that when you're free, your true creativity, your true self, comes out.* 99

TINA TURNER, singer, songwriter, actor, in *Ebony* in 1986

MEDITATION

I release all things that are holding me back from my true self.

REFLECTION

Sis, do you ever feel like there's something holding you back from being your true self? If so, you must figure out what it is and let it go. Whether it's your insecurities, fears, or doubts, you must not let negativity—including your thoughts and the people you surround yourself with—prevent you from being the best version of yourself. Thus, being proactive about pursuing freedom of expression and creativity is a necessity for your self-care journey.

For Black women, a lot of negativity may be holding us back from being our true selves. First off, it's the fear of judgment from people who are not kinfolk. Our hypervisibility and invisibility cause us to simultaneously worry about being seen as a negative stereotype and grimace at the idea of people ignoring our fabulous existence. In addition, society places roles on us we didn't ask for, such as the Competent Colleague at work whose wins get ignored because her employer is trying to quietly fire her (a.k.a. not providing adequate support so that she is eventually pushed out of the organization). These things are exhausting to experience and cause psychological warfare.

To free yourself from any negativity that is preventing you from being your true self, you will have to make time to reflect on what exactly is holding you back. Is it your relationships, work environment, thoughts, or something else? Only you can uncover the truth of that. Moreover, you will have to acknowledge whatever is holding you back, take responsibility for engaging with it, and create a plan to let it go.

Take Action

Evaluate your life. Is there any negativity that is holding you back from being your true self? Take steps to free yourself from it.

Look for Representation

MEDITATION

Seeking out others who look like
me is beneficial for my soul.

REFLECTION

For Black girls and women, representation matters. We need to
be able to see ourselves doing extraordinary things in the world
to believe that we can also do it. However, sometimes it's hard
to find that representation. You must seek it out. Because a lot
of spaces in this world are predominantly white, seeing a Black
person thrive in environments we were once excluded from is
a motivating experience.

For example, for years the science, technology, engineer-
ing, and mathematics (STEM) fields were predominantly known
to be spaces for white men. However, due to increased representation from Black women (and women in general), organizations like Black Girls Code have been able to help increase the
representation for Black women and girls in STEM. Increased

representation in traditionally gatekept spaces means an influx of Black women will have access to information and resources that can lead to greater opportunities for success.

To find the representation you need, start by seeking out Black organizations that may be associated with your intended or current profession. These spaces exist in most fields because Black people need their sacred spaces to gather both within and outside their corporate jobs. Representation doesn't only have to exist in your career field. It can also be on the movie or TV screen or even in the government. Seeing Black women inhabit spaces we were once left out of because of the color of our skin is remarkable and will remind you that anything is possible.

Take Action

Search right now for people who look like you or who are working toward or have accomplished a goal of yours.

Accept Life's Mistakes

If you can't make a mistake,
you can't make anything.

MARVA COLLINS, educator

MEDITATION

Mistakes are lessons that redirect
me to a better path.

REFLECTION

High-functioning, anxious Black women, check in. Does perfectionism have a hold on you? (Of course it does.) Then you need to embrace the power of making mistakes. *Aht, aht.* Don't turn the page. You need this reflection.

Trying to be perfect is your anxiety girl bossing her way through your mind, body, and soul. To you, practicing perfectionism is how you protect your emotions from unexpected circumstances. But really, all you're doing is reinforcing the idea in yourself that you lack self-trust. You don't trust yourself to be able to handle the uncomfortable emotions that come with the unknown. And because most Black women are high achievers, making a mistake is not something you are comfortable with, so you embrace trying to do everything perfectly. When really, you need to learn to accept that you will make mistakes in life, and it is okay. Re-read the Embrace Life's Imperfections meditation for additional guidance in accepting this fact.

Additionally, the world does not like to give us second chances, so we often feel the pressure to get it right the first time. Whew. However, now it's time to let go of that way of thinking. Lean into making mistakes as a way for you to reclaim your power. The best part about embracing making mistakes is that it opens the door for you to radically accept yourself and find inner peace. You'll learn that mistakes do not define you. The way you recover from a mistake does. After all, they are lessons that can redirect you to a better or different path.

Take Action
Think about the lessons that past mistakes have taught you. Write them down.

Unlock Your Greatness

❝ Never underestimate the power of dreams and the influence of the human spirit. We are all the same in this notion: The potential for greatness lives within each of us. ❞

WILMA RUDOLPH, world-record-holding Olympic track and field champion

Greatness lives within me, and I have the power to release it.

Never underestimate the power of your dreams and your ability to pursue those dreams. Greatness is not just a state of being; it's who you are. The power to reach your highest potential does live within you. You just must believe you can access it. After all, you do have that Black Girl Magic.

As a Black woman, you may have been discouraged most of your life to not chase after your wildest dreams. That's because society tends to impose its limited beliefs on us. Shake it off. What others think about your potential is none of your business. You must stay focused on all that you want to achieve.

Unlocking your greatness or highest capabilities to reach your goals starts with your mind. Clear out any negative thoughts, feelings, and beliefs you may have about yourself. This can be done through meditation or positive affirmations combined with deep breathing. (For more guidance, read or revisit the Get Real with Your Growth meditation.) Next, brainstorm how you can reach your desired goal. Make it realistic. It's important that you have small attainable goals as you work toward your big accomplishment. Then, keep track of all your wins to stay motivated. You will see that in no time, you will reach your desired goals—unlocking your greatness.

Take Action

**What do you feel is great about yourself?
Reflect on this question and how these great things
can help you reach your goals.**

Be Proud of Yourself

> *Don't wait until you've reached your goal to be proud of yourself. Be proud of every step you take toward reaching that goal.*

SIMONE BILES, Olympic gymnast

I am allowed to be proud of every step I take toward my goals.

REFLECTION

A healthy dose of pride is good for you. It's a great motivator to help you continue moving forward toward your goals. You see, being satisfied with yourself, your actions, and your accomplishments means your self-esteem is high. However, if you've got a harsh inner critic, it can be a struggle to find the capacity to be proud of yourself for anything that you do—big or small. If you can relate to this, let's work on changing that.

To be more self-assured and at peace with yourself, you'll have to learn how to self-validate. Often, we seek external reassurance from others because we lack self-confidence and self-trust. Perhaps you didn't have the most supportive caregivers growing up, so you never received any words of encouragement and now you don't know how to hype yourself up. Or as a Black woman, maybe you've experienced being put down by peers at work, school, etc., and that made you question your ability to achieve anything.

The truth is, you don't have to wait for anybody to give yourself the love and support you deserve. Being proud of yourself, whether it's with the goals you've reached or are attempting to reach, or just who you are as a person, requires you to be vulnerable with yourself. Get real. Figure out your truest desires and insecurities about getting them. Then, take tiny actionable steps toward reaching these goals. And as you complete each step, reward yourself however you want. You deserve to feel loved and supported by your biggest cheerleader: yourself.

Take Action

Think about something you want to achieve. What are three actionable steps you can complete this month that will bring you closer to your goal and make you proud of yourself?

" Don't wait until you've reached your goal to be proud of yourself.

BE PROUD

of every step you take toward reaching that

GOAL. "

SIMONE BILES,
Olympic gymnast

Pay Attention to Your Self-Image

> *Whatever we believe about ourselves and our ability comes true for us.*

SUSAN L. TAYLOR, journalist, editor-in-chief of *Essence* (1981–2000)

MEDITATION

My mind is a powerful tool for unlocking my capabilities.

REFLECTION

It is so important to pay attention to your self-image because how you view yourself in your mind will reflect in your everyday life. This is because the mind is a very powerful tool. Do not forget that. If you are always talking smack about yourself and putting yourself down, don't be surprised if you're not able to accomplish any of your goals. Why would you be motivated? Your mind has been beaten down by itself to think that it's not capable of completing tasks. Let's work on flipping the script in your brain.

The truth is, a lot of our life's desires start in the mind. So, it is essential that you try to free your mental space of unkind thoughts surrounding your self-image. To do this, you can try using affirmations to challenge those thoughts. Affirmations are powerful positive statements that you can use to change the way you think and feel about yourself. They will transform your life. And if affirmations aren't your thing, you can talk to a mental health professional or a trusted and safe friend to help you through your harsh thoughts.

As a Black woman, your mind must be a fortress that protects yourself against anything that doesn't align with you. The world's favorite place to attack us is through our minds. Whether it's microaggressions that leave you annoyed and angry or discriminatory remarks that make you feel sad and confused, your mind will always be in the first place that society will try to attack you. Thus, you must take care of your mental health. It's the secret to helping you succeed.

Take Action

Think about what you believe about yourself.
Is it something unkind or limiting? If so, how can you
shift your mind to think better of yourself?

Define Success for Yourself

ALTHEA GIBSON, tennis player, professional golfer,
in *So Much to Live For*

MEDITATION

Choosing how I want to define success
in my life is a power move.

REFLECTION

How you choose to measure your successes in life is up to you.
In a world that defines achievements through material posses-
sions like money, medals, and trophies, it's important that you
resist the need to compare yourself to other people's achievements. Instead, choose how you want to define your success.

For Black women, we kind of have no choice but to choose
how we define our achievements. Often, the goalpost for success is moved for us because *some* people do not want to see
us win. Additionally, measuring your life's success by society's
standards can make you feel bad about your life's decisions.
The world often deems a successful woman to be one who
is married and has kids. However, statistically, many Black

women are highly educated, gainfully employed, and single with no partner or child. In the eyes of some, this is not a win, but to you, it could mean you are thriving. So, you must figure out what winning at life looks like to you and not let your measure of success be dictated by society's standards.

To discover how you want to define your success, you will have to reflect on your values and honor them. Moreover, you will have to take steps to protect your mental health and prevent the comparison trap...like getting off social media. Embrace your life for what it is.

Take Action

Explore what success looks like to you.
How would you define it?

Ask for Help

MEDITATION

Doing it yourself does not equal doing it alone.

REFLECTION

I'll do it myself: the infamous words of a hyperindependent baddie who feels like she can't rely on anyone else but herself. *Points finger at you.* But the truth is, sometimes you just got to do it yourself. However, this doesn't mean that you must do it *alone*.

When you choose to step outside of the dominant culture for anything (career, parenting, schooling, etc.), you will be looked at sideways. People won't know what you're doing. On top of that, you're a Black woman so people are already going to gawk, stare, and not mind their own business. So, make sure you get the right support for your outside-of-the-box ventures.

Choosing to do anything yourself, whether it's an independent creative project or starting your own business, requires the courage to believe and trust in yourself. You are doing something totally different than the norm, and when you go against the wavelength of society, you also have to develop mental strength and be prepared for the unexpected. Having any necessary support is part of being prepared, so don't be afraid to go get it.

Take Action

Spend some time thinking about what kind of support you may need with current or future work and/or personal projects. Reflect on how you can obtain that support.

Find Your Voice

66 Do not desire to fit in.
Desire to oblige yourselves to lead. 99

GWENDOLYN BROOKS, poet, author, teacher, in a commencement
speech for the University of Vermont in 1986

MEDITATION

Finding my voice helps me
reconnect with myself.

REFLECTION

Leaders are changemakers, and if you desire to be a leader, you will have to find your voice. Finding your voice means connecting to your most authentic self. Being connected to the truest version of yourself is part of your self-care journey. Additionally, a leader is not always at the forefront of an issue. A leader can also be someone who knows how to lead with silent strength and power. Finding your voice comes with a lot of responsibility, such as knowing when to use your voice versus knowing when to step back and allow others to lead.

Black women have always been phenomenal thought leaders. If you go through the quotes in this book, you will see all many legends of the mind. It seems like in society, Black women tend to be the voice of reason, the voice of the culture, and the voice of humanity. However, our voices are often silenced and ignored because many people do not believe in the value of what we have to say, despite us usually being right.

To find your voice, you will need to build up your self-esteem and get to know yourself. (Read or revisit the Speak Your Truth meditation.) Take time to discover things like what exactly you are trying to lead and what kind of leader you are. If you are not comfortable speaking to large groups of people, that is okay. Not all leaders are loud; some lead in silence. What matters is that you find your authenticity and stay ahead of the culture.

Take Action

Explore which you are more comfortable with: being a leader or someone who fits in.

Take Care of Yourself for Others

❝ *When you take care of yourself, you're a better person for others. When you feel good about yourself, you treat others better.* ❞

SOLANGE KNOWLES, singer, songwriter, actor

MEDITATION

Taking care of myself makes me a better community member.

REFLECTION

Community care is essential to your wellness journey, and if you want to be an elite member of your community, you must take care of yourself. When we treat ourselves well, we learn how we should treat other people. Research has shown that community care is one of the best ways that Black women practice self-care. We're better when we thrive together. If you struggle with the concept of practicing self-care, perhaps this reflection will encourage you to put your well-being first.

You read it in the Prioritize Your Self-Care meditation and it bears repeating: One of the main reasons you may not practice self-care is the belief that you do not have time for it. *Aht, aht.* Try again. You always have time to practice self-care, even if it's only for two to five minutes a day. It's about prioritizing your wellness needs over anything else. If you struggle with wanting to practice self-care, even for just two minutes a day, you must ask yourself the following: *Why do I not think that I am worthy and deserving of care that will nourish my mind, body, and soul? Oop.*

The thing about taking care of yourself is that it teaches you how to love other people. When you choose to practice self-care, it is also community care. This is because practicing self-care is a form of intergenerational healing. You taking care of yourself encourages others to do the same. For so long, Black women have not been allowed or given the self-efficacy to focus on their full well-being. As we are in a self-care renaissance in this current century, it would be foolish not to take advantage of the autonomy you have to put yourself first. Additionally, it'll teach you how to take care of yourself and others. When you love on others, you learn to heal in community and co-regulate to find inner peace.

Take Action
Think of someone you love.
Go plan a self-care day with them.

Reclaim Control of Your Life

❝ You have control over the choices you make. ❞

TARAJI P. HENSON, actor, on NPR's *Tell Me More* in 2009

MEDITATION

My life is a series of choices
that I have control over.

REFLECTION

You are in the driver's seat of your life. The person making all the choices for your life should be you. Of course, there are circumstances either thrown at you or that you just end up in, which you may have no choice over. But while you may not have a choice of enduring these unforeseen situations, you do have a choice of how you handle these circumstances, so keep that in mind when you think about what kind of control you have over your life.

For years, Black women did not have full control over their lives. The women who came before us endured hardships that forced them to make life decisions they may have not chosen, such as who they married or where they lived. *Cough* patriarchy *cough* and redlining *cough*. But now, we have the blessing to make life decisions that align with our truest desires.

Nevertheless, recognizing that you have control over your life choices is a journey, but you do have it. If you struggle with making life decisions, let's talk about how you can become better at making choices. The thing with making choices is that it's not about which choice is better than the other. It's about which choice is right for you, because all choices have consequences. So, lean into that understanding.

Take Action

Think about some of the life choices you've recently made. Do you feel like they align with who you are?

Release Your Past

MEDITATION

Letting go of my past ignites
my future endeavors.

REFLECTION

To move forward in life successfully, you must let go of your past. Of course, this is easier said than done. However, releasing the weight of your previous life experiences creates space for healing and growth. The process of letting go of your past can be challenging, but it is essential to helping you reclaim your power, redefine your narrative, and move forward with purpose.

You may find it hard to move past your previous life experiences because they may have been riddled with traumas and disappointments. These things have a heavy impact on the capacity and capabilities of your mental health. Additionally, for many Black women who obtain success, there is a bit of survivor's guilt. This stems from the fact that some of us come from families where we may be one of the few that *made it out the mud*. Culturally, it is sometimes an expectation that the family member who becomes financially stable may have to assist the rest of the family. However, if you are trying to move forward in life and advance to the next level, you have got to drop the need to look out for everyone else but yourself.

To free yourself from your past and focus on your future, you will have to do some internal work. Start choosing to prioritize your mental health by doing things like self-reflective activities such as journaling. Through writing, you can acknowledge your past pain, explore any limited beliefs, and brainstorm about what's to come.

Take Action

Ask yourself: *What can I do to help myself let go of my past?*

"It isn't **where** you come from, it's where **you're going** that counts."

ELLA FITZGERALD,
jazz singer a.k.a. "Queen of Jazz"

Use Your Support Systems

> **Dreams do come true, but not without the help of others, a good education, a strong work ethic, and the courage to lean in.**

URSULA BURNS, former CEO of Xerox

MEDITATION

I am not afraid to lean into my support system.

REFLECTION

There is nothing wrong with needing help as you fulfill your dreams. Our hearts are wired for connection, and we need community to thrive. As we move through life, of course we can do things alone, but why would we? It is necessary to lean on the support systems around you to help you get further in life. Whether it's access to a good education system, supportive loved ones, or peers with an expansive network, it is important to understand that you need a support system to help you get there, sustain your dream, and push you to new heights.

For Black women, our greatest support system is each other, and it's important to recognize that. But you knew that. Having each other's backs is one of our superpowers. Having a strong support system is great, but if you don't know how to access it or don't like the kind of support you're getting, then what is the point? This is where you need to speak up for yourself. For example, families are one of the biggest supports for college students but can also be the biggest source of anxiety. You have to develop the skill to set boundaries with your family to get the support you need from them. Yes, easier said than done, *ha*.

Additionally, some people don't have strong support systems. If this is you, you can gain access to other systems of support; it will just require you to break out of your shell a bit. Depending on your setting (work, school, community, etc.), start small by attempting to form friendships with people you've met before or seek out resources in your community. Find your support system. It is out there.

Take Action

Consider which support systems you can access right now to help you with your needs.

Learn to Slow Down

66 *Never be afraid to sit awhile and think.* 99

LORRAINE HANSBERRY, playwright, writer

MEDITATION

Allowing myself to slow down is
how I reconnect with myself.

REFLECTION

Sitting a while in silence, inside or outside, is such a great activity (weather permitting). It's also excellent for your physical and mental health. Learning to slow down is an art form because not many of us want to actually do all of that—sit outside and get bit by bugs.

You see, we live in a world where capitalism is at the core of everything we do. It's the driving force for many things that happen in society. It's the reason for hustle culture and why "LLC Twitter" is overrun by Black entrepreneurs. *Ha*. Everybody is trying to get ahead and make their first million dollars.

Nevertheless, you need to learn to slow down before life catches up to you. Slowing down will help you better manage your stress levels, such as the stress from microaggressions and misogynoir. As a reminder, the leading cause of death among Black women in the United States is cardiovascular disease, which can be prevented through mental and physical interventions. These include slowing down activities like sitting outside in the sun, journaling, cooking, deep breathing exercises, and casual walks.

Take Action

When's the last time you sat outside and let the sun hit your face for five minutes? Go do that.

Always Ask Questions

RUBY DEE, actor, poet, playwright, screenwriter,
journalist, civil rights activist

MEDITATION

My curiosity provides me with the clarity I need.

REFLECTION

Let your curiosity be the fire that ignites your self-care journey. Being able to ask questions and get answers that help you
learn and expand your mind is incredibly beneficial for your
mental health. However, not everyone is comfortable with asking questions.

If you grew up in a Black household, you likely experienced
a parent telling you that you were talking back when you were
simply asking valid questions. This can make it hard for you to
ask necessary questions in any scenario, leading you to either
make assumptions or have anxious thoughts that don't easily
go away.

To go far in life, you've got to be curious and inquisi-
tive. There are no bad questions. When you ask questions,
you always gain clarity. It's important to seek clarity versus

confusion. Confusion is where all the red flags for that situationship thrive, whereas clarity fills you with peace, calm, and clear direction. Follow the calm and ask those questions, because asking the right questions will lead you to the door for other opportunities.

Asking questions also opens the door for healing within you and others, because it provides space for things like reflection, understanding, and even correction with thoughts and behaviors. There are many different types of questions, one of them being open-ended. Instead of asking someone a direct yes or no question, you can ask them to describe a fun fact about themselves. You can also pose these types of questions to yourself during mindful activities like journaling and painting.

Take Action

If you're afraid to ask other people questions, explore that in your journal. If you're not afraid to ask other people questions, ask yourself this: *What is something I need clarity on in my life?*

Step Away from What's Familiar

" To soar toward what's possible, you must leave behind what's comfortable. "

CICELY TYSON, actor, in *Just as I Am: A Memoir*

MEDITATION

It is safe for me to let go of what I am familiar with for the unknown.

REFLECTION

When was the last time you walked away from something familiar for something new and unknown? The things that we are familiar with are like lovely hugs, making us feel warm and secure. However, eventually the hug must end, and you must move on. Outside of what you're used to lie many roads that can help lead you to success. So, what is holding you back from leaving your current familiar space to chase your goals?

To soar toward your goals, you will have to step away from what you're comfortable with. It's so easy to get caught up in following one path toward your desired achievements, but the truth is there are many roads that lead to one destination—your desired goal. As a Black woman, you have no choice but to live outside of what you know. Your hypervisibility makes others see you, and your invisibility makes others not see you, so you have to get real comfortable with yourself and with the uncomfortable, which you are most likely an expert at.

If you struggle with doing things outside of your norm, try something small first. Perhaps wear a different hairstyle, take a different route to work, or wear different pairs of earrings than you normally do. If trying new things outside of what you know gives you anxiety, take it slow. There's no rush to stepping outside of the box where you're comfortable. Stay there, and in time, you'll be ready to leave your cocoon and fly like a butterfly. For further encouragement, re-read the Leave Your Comfort Zone meditation earlier in this book.

Take Action

When was the last time you did something new? If not recently, go do something different! Reflect on how this made you feel.

Remember Your Big Dreams

❝ *When your dreams are bigger than the places you find yourself in, sometimes you need to seek out your own reminders that there is more.* ❞

ELAINE WELTEROTH, journalist, editor, author, television host, in *More Than Enough: Claiming Space for Who You Are (No Matter What They Say)*

MEDITATION

I am reminded that my dreams are never too big.

REFLECTION

Your dreams are never too big for this world. If there is something in your heart that you desire to achieve, don't be afraid to go after it. Sometimes our current circumstances do not reflect what we want our future to be, but that is okay. Seek out things that help you remember you have bigger goals to achieve.

As a Black woman, you need reminders about your dreams because sometimes your goals can feel extremely far away. We live in a world that always throws a ton of obstacles in front of Black women as we try to achieve our goals. Forget those hurdles and stay focused on your desired accomplishment.

To remind yourself of your big dreams, get a journal where you can write about your goals and muse about how you envision your future life. A journal is a great way to keep track of your dreams because you can look back and see how your goals have changed and the steps you've taken toward them. The journal you use can be handwritten or typed up in your phone or computer.

Another way to remind yourself of your goals is to check in with people you trust who know about your plans. These people will hold you accountable and help you make those tiny, attainable steps toward your big goal. Go get 'em, girl.

Take Action

Think about your big dreams. Go search for the reminder that there is more out there.

169

Know When to Move Forward

MEDITATION

I pay attention to where I am in my personal growth journey.

REFLECTION

The key to growing as a person is knowing when to move forward, take a step back, or stand still. Take this moment to think about where you are in your personal growth journey. Do you need to push forward, chill out, or take a break? If you are in the "move forward" stage, you may have to make choices for yourself about where you are going. For instance, is it further along your healing journey, or are you exiting your current path to try something new?

Now, this doesn't only apply to a wellness journey; it can apply to anything, like your career path. Raise your hand if you have ever been at work and realized that the only way to grow professionally was to leave that job! For many Black women, moving forward in our careers usually means exiting stage left without taking a bow, especially in the corporate space.

Ultimately, it's important to pay attention to where you are in your personal or professional growth journey. You need to know what your next move is supposed to be. And especially if you are a Black woman, you have to stay ahead of the curve in the corporate space because some colleagues will not think twice about doing everything they can to get you to quietly quit.

Take Action

Knowing when to exit a situation is a power move and a way of moving forward. Are there any circumstances that you need to leave behind? Think about it.

Recognize Your Inner Magic

“ *Where there is a woman there is magic.* ”

NTOZAKE SHANGE, playwright, poet,
in *Sassafrass, Cypress & Indigo: A Novel*

MEDITATION

My magical power is that I am a Black woman.

REFLECTION

Women are magical, especially Black women. *Period.* It's very important that you recognize your inner magic as you move through the world. The magic I speak of as a Black woman is our ability to adapt, create, and inspire. We are the code-switching queens, and that is okay. Because, uh, you can't bring the full you to your job, so they get a version of you that only exists from nine to five, Monday through Friday.

Recognizing your inner magic is actually quite the journey. You see, from childhood, you were probably fed messages telling you that you are less than, that you are not desirable, that you're not attractive, that the way you look is not natural, and just all the things that negate your natural existence in this world.

As you get older, you go through life and experience what we'll call your *Black Womanhood Awakening*. It's that point in your adulthood, often in your mid-twenties, where you realize: *Ohh, I was never ugly. I was never undesirable. Nothing was ever wrong with me. It's just that the environments I was in, where I was the only one, did not want me there.*

Now, this may apply more to individuals who grew up in mainly non-Black spaces, but having a reckoning with your identity and who you are in this world still exists regardless of your childhood experiences. If you've never had this epiphany, this awakening, and the acceptance of your identity, know that it will eventually happen and that it is not a destination but a journey. A journey of self-exploration and self-discovery.

Discovering your magic is about connecting with your humanity as a Black woman. It is your superpower. To recognize that your positive attributes despite others trying to demean your existence. It's how you reclaim your power in a world determined to make you hate yourself. This is how you resist. You gladly stand tall and declare, "I am magical, and every natural thing about me is beautifully perfect just the way it is."

Take Action

Reflect on what you love the most about being a Black woman.

"Where there is a 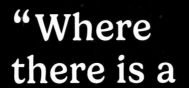 there is magic."

NTOZAKE SHANGE,
playwright, poet, in *Sassafrass, Cypress & Indigo: A Novel*

Use Your Strength to Heal

❝ I am stronger than I am broken. ❞

ROXANE GAY, writer, professor, editor, social
commentator, in *Hunger: A Memoir of (My) Body*

MEDITATION

My strength is my healing superpower.

REFLECTION

The "strong Black woman" trope is out; however, it is okay
to recognize that you do have inner strength. The power you
possess on the inside helps you get through challenging times.
Let's be real   life can sometimes really kick your butt. You will
face situations that try to break your spirit, and sometimes they
will, leaving you to put the pieces of your life back together.
Although what you go through may try to bring you to the darkness of depression, you can acknowledge that *you are stronger than you are broken*. Whatever trauma you endured is not
your fault. Nobody was there to protect you, but now you are
your own protector.

When healing from trauma, it's important to remember
that everybody's healing timeline is different. Trauma healing
asks a lot from you, so be gentle with yourself and establish

safety—safety within yourself, with others, and in your environment. If needed, contact a mental health professional to accompany you on your healing journey. Most importantly, let the healing process guide you back to yourself as you strip away the layers of trauma that tried to break you.

In addition, if you do not feel like you have trauma to heal from, you can still use your inner strength to help navigate your wellness journey. Using your strength to heal is ultimately about not being afraid to harness your emotional power to push yourself forward to a higher sense of self.

Take Action

When was the last time you experienced something that tried to break your spirit? Reflect on how you pulled through.

Uncover Family Stories

CHARMAINE WILKERSON, journalist, writer, author, in *Black Cake: A Novel*

MEDITATION

Connecting to my family's ancestral lineage empowers my spirit.

REFLECTION

It is important to know where you come from. Building a connection to your family's history and journeying back to your roots allows you to get a sense of belonging and understanding. Uncovering your family's stories can also help shine a light on things that you may have been wondering about.

In many Black families, to gather information you will have to go to an elder like a parent or grandparent. Be prepared, though—they may not be forthcoming with the information. What is so remarkable about the way families work is that you do not have to know the stories to be impacted by them. This is known as intergenerational trauma, where events that happened in the previous generation result in behaviors and traumas passed down to the next, such as spanking children or poor conflict resolution skills.

Additionally, many Black women have complex backgrounds. Some of us are descendants of enslaved people with a fragmented connection to the Motherland of Africa. Others are mixed, daughters of Black immigrants, Afro-Latina, etc. Nonetheless, we are all still connected.

This reflection has one goal: connecting you to where you come from and unveiling all the many layers that make up your identity. You don't have to visit Africa to gain a better connection to your roots. It's about going back to where your family was raised and created their community.

Hopefully, after you make space for yourself to reflect on your family's story, you will have a greater sense of pride. As Black women, we come from a strong lineage of people who survived and thrived despite all the atrocities they endured because of colonization, such as enslavement, segregation, and mistreatment (like our bodies being used as experiments for advancements in healthcare).

Take Action

If you're in contact with any elder family members, give them a call to hear a bit of their life's story.

Understand Your Self-Worth

MEDITATION

Knowing my self-worth is the key to my inner peace.

REFLECTION

Let us talk about self-worth. The world is a materialistic place. Society will try to attach a value to you based on your appearance, your tax bracket, and your relationship status. It is important to stay grounded in yourself and know that your worth is not connected to your physical attributes, bank account, or marital status. Your self-worth is based on what you think of yourself and the value you have for your well-being. Not how the world views you. Knowing your self-worth will help you maintain your self-care journey.

As Black women, we must not care about what this world thinks about us because we already know—y'all don't like us. Which quite frankly makes no sense because we are an immaculate species. Trendsetters and changemakers. *Okurrr!* However, our humanity is often disregarded, and we are commodified for our ability to provide support and care to others. Thus, you must not seek validation from society. Your validation must come from within, and a little love from people you trust and love doesn't hurt either.

Nonetheless, if you struggle with low self-worth, you will need to build up your self-confidence. This can include challenging any negative thoughts with positive affirmations, getting off social media so you do not compare yourself to your peers, and setting small attainable goals that you know you will complete to boost your self-esteem. It's important that you learn your self-value comes from within and not from external pressures that you or the world places on you. You are inherently valuable because you exist. The world may make you think that to be respected and valued, you must act a certain way or present yourself a certain way to society. Leaning into respectability politics or the cultural and social demands of dominant culture (white supremacy and patriarchy) will not garner your personhood the value you crave from others and the world.

Take Action

Take a moment to think about yourself. How do you feel about your self-worth?

Follow Your Conscience

I did what my conscience told me to do, and you can't fail if you do that.

ANITA HILL, lawyer, educator, author

MEDITATION

It's always a good idea to listen to my conscience.

REFLECTION

Stay true to who you are by listening to your conscience. Your conscience is your moral compass, helping you decide between what is morally right or wrong according to your standards. No matter the outcome of a situation, good or bad, it is always beneficial to listen to what your mind is telling you to do. When you honor your conscience, you stay true to your values as a person. And when you do, you will reduce your stress and connect more to your authentic self.

If you feel like you are not the best at respecting your conscience, take some time to reflect on that. It's important to explore why you have a hard time honoring your own moral code. Could it be years of conditioning from society that made you feel like, as a Black woman, you don't really have a say in what goes on inside your body? *Sigh.* If so, that will need to be explored. The world (ahem, physicians) loves to make us feel like we are guests in our own bodies and that they know best. It's distressing and can be a catalyst for feeling disconnected from your body.

It's time for you to reconnect with yourself. Reclaim your mind, body, and soul back by choosing to actively honor your conscience.

Take Action

Explore with yourself. Are you good at listening to your conscience? If yes, how so? If no, how come?

Manage Your Stress

❝ *It's not the load that breaks you down; it's the way you carry it.* ❞

LENA HORNE, singer, actor, dancer, civil rights activist

MEDITATION

I inhale peace and exhale stress.

REFLECTION

Toxic stress is something that Black women deal with at a higher rate. Studies have shown that stress is the leading cause of major illnesses like cardiovascular disease, which is one of the leading causes of death in Black women. The solution: learn to better manage your stress before it becomes toxic and harms your health.

Now, the fact is, you can't really avoid *all* stressors. That would be wonderful, but it's not realistic. Instead, it's important that you become aware of things that might stress you out and take whatever steps are possible to manage that. For example, interacting with a coworker who perpetuates microaggressions is a stressor, and as a step, you can try to stay away from that person.

Over here in the Oludara Adeeyo universe, we like to focus on the mind, body, and soul. You will need coping skills for these three areas when it comes to managing stress. Some examples include setting boundaries with family, going on a long walk, and practicing radical honesty with yourself. Whatever you decide to do, make sure you incorporate your self-care skills into your daily routine—start small, but be consistent. Practicing coping skills will become instinctual and encourage better emotional regulation. This way, if you encounter an unexpected racist situation, like someone assuming you work at a grocery store even though you're not in a uniform, the elevated emotions will not last long and won't turn into toxic stress.

Get started on building your stress management toolkit as soon as possible. You never know when you just might need your newly learned coping skills.

Take Action

Be honest with yourself: How are you managing your stress?

Try New Things

MEDITATION

Trying new things is good for
my mind, body, and soul.

REFLECTION

Trying new things should be an integral part of your self-care journey. Whether it's new food, a language, an event, or a hobby, doing something for the first time is exciting and stimulating for your mind, body, and soul. So, when's the last time you tried something new? Here's why you should absolutely try switching things up...

First off, the journey of trying new things is a path of self-discovery. You need to be open to endless possibilities of enlightenment, where you will learn more about what you like and don't like. Reconnecting with and having a better understanding of yourself is key to maintaining your well-being. Additionally, let's say you're learning a new skill or a language where, at first, you'll have no idea what you're doing. The more you do it, the better you'll get. Through these kinds of activities, you'll improve your mental health and increase your cognitive functioning, enabling your mind to quickly bounce back from any emotional injuries caused by things like microaggressions.

To get started on trying something new, you must simply just do it. Think about an area in your life that you feel could use more excitement and go from there. And if you're still unsure of where to start, try something as easy as switching up your hairstyle—like those boho knotless braids you've been curious about.

Take Action

Think about it: When's the last time you tried something new—and how did it go?

Index

About the Author

OLUDARA ADEEYO is a mental health therapist and the author of *Self-Care for Black Women; Affirmations for Black Women: A Journal;* and *Mind, Body, & Soul: A Self-Care Coloring Book for Black Women.* She is passionate about helping people, especially Black women, improve their overall wellness. Before becoming a licensed clinical social worker, Oludara worked as a writer and editor. She has been an associate web editor at *Cosmopolitan* and the managing editor at *XXL.* Oludara lives in Los Angeles.